Lord Restore My Soul

PERSONAL REFLECTIONS FROM THE PSALMS

By

DAVID KNIGHT

CONTENTS

A WAITING LOVE, A LOVE THAT DOES NOT CONTROL
1
ACCOUNTABILITY IN LIFE CAN BE PAINFUL
4
ANGUISHED CRY OF A WEEPING SOUL
7
ANSWER ME DO NOT HIDE FROM ME
10
ASCRIBE DRAWS EVER INWARD
12
BELIEF IS THE LIFE BLOOD OF FAITH
15
BLESSED WORDS OF LOVE
18
CAPSTONE OF LOVE
21
COME FEED ON THE FOOD OF LOVE AND THE OIL OF JOY
23
CONFESSION IS THE GATEWAY TO FREEDOM
27
CONTENTMENT OF THE HEART IS THE FIBRE OF FAITH
31

DARK NIGHT BECAME DAWN OF LOVE
37
DEEP ROOTS OF GOD'S LOVE
42
DELIGHT YOURSELF IN THE AWE OF GOD'S CREATION
45
DESIRE FOR GOD'S JOY
47
DO NOT BE ANGRY; SEEK GOD'S LOVE
49
EMOTIONS ARE A BEACON TO OUR SOUL
52
FACE OF LOVE
55
FORGIVENESS IS THE KEY TO GOD'S HEART!
59
FRAGRANT LOVE RESPONDS TO THE CALL OF LOVE
62
FREEING BREATH OF JOY
67
GLORIOUS THINGS ARE SAID OF YOU
70
GOD BLESSED THE WORDS SPOKEN
73
GOD RESTED; WHY DON'T WE?
75
GODS JOYFUL MERCY
78
GOD'S DOORKEEPER
80
GOD'S LOVE REDEEMS THE REPENTANT
83
GOD'S TRUTH IS THE WAY
86
GRACE- MESSAGE THAT BLOOMS
88
HE MAKES ME LIE DOWN IN GREEN PASTURES
91

HEARTACHE OF SELF- LOVE CRUSHES THE SPIRIT
94
I WILL TAKE REFUGE IN THE SHADOW OF YOUR WINGS
96
IN OUR DARKEST MOMENT THE LIGHT WITHIN IS OUR SENTINEL OF LOVE
99
IN YOU LORD I BREATHE THE FRAGRANCE OF LOVE
102
JOYFUL FOREST BATHING IMMERSED IN THE SPIRIT OF GOD
107
LET THERE BE LIGHT
111
LOST HEART IN A WORLD OF ME-ISMS
114
MAJESTY OF GOD'S POWER IS SEEN AT THE PEAK
117
MY HEART PULSES WITH DESIRE
120
O LORD, YOU ARE MY GOD
124
PASSAGE OF ADULTHOOD
127
REFLECTION OF DIVINE GLORY
130
SENIOR WITNESS OF INNER LOVING LIGHT
137
SILENCE AND SOLITUDE; THE TWIN BEAMS TO DIVINE LOVE
141
THANKFUL HEART OF LIGHT COVERS THE BLADE OF DARKNESS
146
THE COMFORTER EMBRACES THE CONTROLLER
149

THE GIFT OF LIFE IS GOD'S LOVE TO US
154
THE PATH OF LOVE
157
TOO BUSY TO LISTEN
160
TRUST IS THE OPEN DOOR TO GOD'S PEACE
163
WHAT IS PRAYER?
166
WISDOM OF LOVING SILENCE
170

A WAITING LOVE, A LOVE THAT DOES NOT CONTROL

I wait for the Lord, my soul waits. And in his word, I put my hope. My soul waits for the Lord more than the watchmen wait for the morning. Psalm 130:5

The other day I spent all morning waiting in a place I rather not be. There was pain within me that cried for attention. I was scared and feeling very much sorry for myself! I was in the Emergency unit of the Hospital. After a flurry of blood samples, X-rays, and E.C.G's, I was left to wait. Wait I did! I had no choice, so I sat and observed and thought.

I was sitting in a corner, in the shadows by the ambulance entrance. I watched as patients were brought in, how they were placed, how the nurses determined where they should go, how the specialists came in and gave instructions. All was spoken in muted language. I became aware of the urgency to relieve the patient of pain and make their suffering more manageable and bearable. What interested me the most was how the patient reacted to their situation! There was quiet resignation, there was stoicism with wet tears, there was anger and hostility that produced a contrary attitude and there was a deep fear that expressed itself through body and facial tensions. It is difficult to give up control of your life, especially to others!

I am anxious, hypersensitive and impatient! To wait for 6 hours was eternity. Yet I was living in a reality that there was nothing I can do but become a waiting person. In my angst for calmness wrapped itself around my soul as the Holy Spirit reminded me that my soul is waiting for the Lord. My waiting became shaped by my alertness to his Word. I knew that this hope would sustain me and guide me through the uncertainty of this moment. I was experiencing a love, that I could not control; all I could do was hold onto the hand of Jesus who guides me through my darkness of loneliness and fear of uncertainties. In a sense I found I was giving up my control over my future and allowing God to define my life. Instead of "wishing" what might be I found I was living in the "hope" of his love and promises. I discerned a fundamental truth that rather than me be the initiator of all things I must learn to being the recipient of other people's initiatives. Here I realized is the greatest mystery of all whether in work, in love, in sickness, in friendship, in community there is the aspect of waiting. It is precisely in this waiting that the intensity of friendship and love is revealed.

It is when I most alone waiting upon the Lord that the passion of God's love shines through. He reminds me I am not alone and his mystical hand presses firmly on my shoulder reassuring me of his presence. Like the morning mist that evaporates before the warm rays of the dawn sun so God's love dissipates my self-pity to rejoice before the joy of the Son's presence in my heart. What is truly amazing my narcissism is transformed to compassion for those who are hurting and are in pain. This is what happened the longer I waited the more I became sensitive to the needs of those around me and I felt their agony more deeply. The love of God within me intensified as I quietly prayed for God's mercy, compassion and care for them.

I walked into the Emergency with the fear of death in my heart but left with God's love deeply entrenched in my heart instead. The waiting had shown me that his love is a love you cannot control for he is in control of my life. It was indeed a timely reminder!

ACCOUNTABILITY IN LIFE CAN BE PAINFUL

"I have sinned against the Lord" [2 Samuel 12:13]." Against you only have I sinned and done what is evil in your sight" [Psalm 51:4]. The sacrifices of God are a broken spirit; a broken and contrite heart" [Psalm 51:17]. I live in a high and lowly place but also with him who is contrite and lowly in spirit to revive the spirit of the lowly and to revive the heart of the contrite... I have seen his ways but will heal him. I will guide him and restore comfort to him [Isaiah 57:15, 18] "I have sinned for I have betrayed innocent blood" Matthew 27:4

Accountability in life is painful as it is avoided. We know when we have sinned; the depth of guilt in our soul constantly drags us to a depressive state until we acknowledge our sin before God. When we do sin there are consequences. Relationship with God, relationship with friends and family and relationship with us are broken. There is discord and division. Committed sin is like a cancer that eats and slowly destroys the soul.

Just like Adam and Eve who sinned and hid themselves from each other and from God but could not; so we cannot hide from our sin. Eventually we will be held accountable; there is no escape. David found this out when faced with Nathan's charge. His passion and lust destroyed a life and created a life. I have sinned against the Lord was David's response. In David's case his response was genuine his contriteness of spirit was intense; he had upset the Lord and David grieved that he had caused the Lord, who he loved to move to anger. There had to be a judgment for this sin: the Lord decreed that because a life had been taken; so he will take the life of the one that had been conceived in sin. Who can grasp the horror that Judas Iscariot must have felt when he said I have sinned for I have betrayed innocent blood! He just had seen Jesus, the Son of God, arrested, beaten and taken away for a bag of Coin. We will never know for sure what motivated him to commit this dastardly act; what we do know he could not live with himself after the sin was committed; he committed suicide! While Jesus cross was the cross of new life to come; Judas cross was the cross of death.

When I reflect on these two events it leaves me with a profound realization that I can take sin too easily. I am talking about the small daily sins that occur: gossiping, lies, slander, envy, anger, lustful thoughts and pride. I confess from time to time my lips, my thoughts and my actions do sin. Do I feel guilt? Is there contriteness in my heart? Sadly, not always! I wish when I do sin my spirit was truly sorry and contrite. I will watch my ways and keep my tongue from sin; I will put a muzzle on my mouth.... but when I was silent and still not even saying anything good, my anguish increased. [Psalm 39:1-2]. There are times my attitude is one of déjà vu. Why is this? What causes this spirit of indifference and inertia? The thought that comes to mind is how much do I love myself, how much do I love my neighbor and how much do I love my God? The more we walk in the shadows with our back to our Savior to more we are likely to sin. God our savior radiates love and abhors sin. We cannot live in both worlds. The more we know and believe that we are loved and never alone the more we are likely to walk pass the opportunities to sin because of our love and passion for God. Our spirit is bound by the grace of God; that gives us freedom to be who we are meant to be. To live in total abandonment is to be bound by sin!

The other thought that comes to mind is that we often do not take God's judgment seriously enough. It seems to me the guiltier we are the more our ears are deaf to the consequences of sin! Paul quotes in Romans: the wages of sin is death. Why? The more indifferent we are to sin the more our hearts become harden to the love of God and the more we hate ourselves. Even though we do not recognize it the silent word of God's judgment is within us.

ANGUISHED CRY OF A WEEPING SOUL!

In my anguish I cried to the Lord and he answered by setting me free (Psalm18:5)

I have great sorrow and unceasing anguish in my heart (Romans 9:2)

We are consumed by your anger and terrified by your indignation (Psalm 90:7)

An angry man stirs up dissension and a hot tempered one commits many sins (Proverbs 29:22)

He who conceals his hatred has lying lips and whoever spread slander is a fool (Proverbs 10:18)

If I say I love god but hates his brother he is a liar (1 John 4:20)

Wisdom is found on the lips of the discerning (Proverb 10:3)

Fear of the Lord adds length to life (Proverb 10:27)

Hope deferred makes the heart sick but a longing fulfilled is tree of life (Proverbs 13:12)

Then those who have fallen asleep in Christ are lost (1 Corinthians 15:18)

Jesus wept (John 11:35)

Each and every day my heart becomes heavier and heavier for the darkness that is spreading over this world lies deeply embedded in my heart for the spirit of anger, anguish and fear torment my soul to such a point that the spirit of love, grace and hope lie hidden in its shadow. Comforting words like God is in control; God is with you; God is love remain in the darkest corners of my angst. All I can do is simply weep inwardly. I know my issue is not a lack of meekness for I am nothing compared to my God but rather the deep sense of foreboding is entrenching into every core of my soul. Every new day my muscles ache more, my burden feels heavier! I sense the world is turning towards a dark new dawn of violence, hatred, intolerance and anger.

Words of anger, bitterness and hatred which are full of vitriol have been unleashed on the masses which have woken up their unfilled rights and entitlements and with righteous voice they call for action to satisfy their Me-ism desires. The true states of their hearts are exposed! They hate the neighbour. There is no love in their hearts. They seek to follow the Gods of materialism and need. The spirit of revenge to take back what they believe is theirs is becoming a spiritual manta. The people of faith speak the words of love but their hearts are void of love; their faith are acts akin to sleep walking grace. Love is gone; only hypocrisy lies on the lips.

History has shown repeatedly that when the fuel of dissent and discord is thrown at the masses a flaming inflammation takes over which cannot be controlled easily as anarchy, violence, and revengeful actions create death, chaos and mayhem! All because of the pride and lust for leaders to satisfy their own egos and agendas.

When love of neighbour is transformed to neighbour is my enemy; love retreats to a spirit of fear and totalitarianism. This is what saddens my spirit. It is the anguish of my soul that I feel powerless as I watch once again a world disintegrating where the gun becomes the arbiter of the law of the land. All I can do is pray for God mercy and for Wisdom which is found on the lips of the discerning

The dark clouds of Mordor are on the ascendency as the Christian saints are asleep at the switch drenched in the stupor of their Me-isms and their Materialistic spirit! My soul indeed weeps.

ANSWER ME DO NOT HIDE FROM ME

Answer me, O Lord out of goodness of your love; in your great mercy turn to me. Do not hide your face from your servant [Psalm 69:16]. Then they cried out to the Lord in their trouble, and he saved them from their distress. He sent forth his word and healed them. Lord, let them give thanks to the Lord for his unfailing love [Psalm 107:19-21]

Children love to play hide and seek. Nothing delights them more than when they are found, and the sooner the better. Their impatience to be found leads them to make sounds, or quickly jump out of their hiding place and back so the "seeker" can discover them quickly. When discovered there is much delight and laughter. Distress quickly occurs, however, if they are not found or are discovered by someone who is not part of the game. Hide and seek is a game that illustrates well our desire to belong and hence to be discovered. Not to be found illustrates our fear of abandonment and isolation.

When the psalmist cries to the Lord – not to hide his face – he is feeling alone and seeks company. The paradox is that the Lord is always there, like the father of the prodigal son. He is waiting for us to turn to him. It is an impediment in our heart that creates shame, or fear that is a consequence of a sin we have committed. By this action God is not with us, even though he is still within us. We need to act in repentance and contrition to receive the merciful forgiveness of a loving father-and so we –cry out to the Lord in our trouble- and like a tender father he shows his love and embrace by sending his "word and heals" us.

What is this word he sends? It is the one – I am the way, and the truth, and the life - it is his son Jesus Christ who is the very essence of love. By following his life, obeying his commands we will walk the path of righteousness and goodness. What is meant by heals? It is through believing in Jesus word and desiring to follow his word, that we are empowered by the teacher and the comforter the Holy Spirit. This empowerment occurs when the spirit of grace abides in you; it is as if the Jesus abides in you also. A union of love now exists in you as the spirit of grace and the love of Jesus guide your very thoughts and actions. In this way God is no longer hidden but very much alive in you. Thanks be to God.

ASCRIBE DRAWS EVER INWARD

Ascribe greatness to our God the Rock
His work is perfect
And all his ways are just (Hymn)
Ascribe to the Lord the glory due his name
(Psalm 29:2)

A recent article bemoans the loss of civility with the rise of anything goes with the result of the loss of politeness and the loss of concern for others. The study reported that:

• 86% of Americans reported having been victims of uncivility

• 72% encountered rude behaviour

• 72% worried about children being bullied online

• 69% felt cyber bullying was on the increase

• 50% of children encountered rude behaviour at school

• 45% of 20 years and under were afraid to be teenagers because of uncivil behaviour

With statistics like these is it no wonder, according to the article, that anxiety, insecurity and depression are almost at epidemic levels. Does this data mean our society is in decline? I am tempted to say yes; what I believe is that our freedom which we cherish is very much being abused and is under attack! It is interesting to observe that more network websites are closing the comment window for it is difficult to control because of the growth of abusive "troll" comments and increased hacker activity.

I would further suggest that our society with the advent of the God of Self and it is cousin Anxiety is leading us into a more closed society where trust and hope is fading; where the only response is either regressive passiveness or violent outburst; where ascribing values on anyone is based on shallowness rather than on their depth of their character. Values are based on emotionalism based on what we want to believe about that person rather than on who they really are.

The word ascribe has a deep and interesting history. Fundamentally the word means to "Scratch figures or numbers on a piece of bark or wax; from this the word Shriven followed." As death approached it was important to scratch out the sins of your life by means of confession to a priest who would absolve your sins so in a state of purity you would be better prepared to go to heaven. With the growing demand to record events and decisions scribes would scratch with a styling pen with much artistry, accuracy and acumen. When attributes were credited to a person, values were being ascribed (scratched) to that person that gave a deep and inner meaning about that person. Ascribe greatness was to describe the goodness within that individual. I sense that today when we ascribe values on anyone it reflects our desired perception on how that person makes us feel rather than on their true inner character. This is the consequence of me-ism and shallowness that turns ascribed values inside out from community desired values to individualized values.

The loss of civility and the vanishing heroes are all reflection of a society drawing inwards. We are living in a society that is increasingly become more restless, more angry, and more lawless, where control of restraint is fading before the values of anything goes. If we can get away that's OK.

Ascribe to the Lord the glory due his name is nay impossible in a society just described for the only values that can be ascribed are self-values where greatness and goodness seemed to have no place where shallowness and anxiety co-exist.

BELIEF IS THE LIFE-BLOOD OF FAITH!

Isaiah 53: Who believed my message?

Psalm 3:6 I trust in the Lord

Psalm 56:3 I will trust in the You

Psalm 119:62 I trust in your word

John 20:8 He saw and believed

We do not believe in ourselves until someone reveals that deep inside something is valuable, worth listening to, worthy of our trust, sacred to one's touch once we believe in ourselves we can risk curiosity wonder spontaneous delight or any experience that reveals the human spirit (EE Cummings- American poet, painter, essayist, author)

Why is it so difficult to believe in God, in statements, in ourselves? Part of the problem is we live in a grossly negative world where facts and conclusion change with the speed of machine gun fire; that it is impossible to discern truth, to acquire faith and to develop trust. It is then not surprising that so many live in a void; a faithless vacuum where true relationship is non-existent and hope is a lost cause. Part of the problem is that we live in the cult of "self" where we seek answers through our own values and perceptions which is deadly when fulfillment, trust and love is absent. Perhaps the major issue is our extreme reliance on rationalism and logic; what can be seen and proven must be true. This is fine except what is true today is false tomorrow. It is not surprising we have become a people of doubters and naysayers! In consequence societal values are less seen as the moral arbiters of what is right and wrong that leads both to a discontented attitude and an inward surge towards self for answers! This begs the questions what if I don't believe in myself?

We should note that "Believe" has the same root in Greek as the word faith; namely Pistos; which involves knowledge, and trust. If knowledge is constantly changing trust is shaken and faith is tenuous; this makes belief difficult to cultivate. You might say for belief to exist there must be trust; trust in turn is very much the lifeblood of faith! For me to believe I must trust; but how is this possible when I have spent a lifetime in distrusting myself and others? The words of Cumming speaks so loudly to me: We do not believe in ourselves until someone reveals that deep inside (us there is) something valuable. This is similar to the reaction we receive when the Father says – You are my son in whom I am well pleased! What is implied they are words said by a person who is worthy of our trust and because we trust we can believe in what is said. In these words of affirmation said out of love and concern doubt is replaced by trust; and from this initial trust of believing a life of faith can grow!

My faith in the Lord grows daily for his words are trustworthy; my belief in friend have grown because their words are backed by their actions; and my belief in self has grown as I spend time in silence before the Lord.

When I look at my Lord I believe for I see someone who loves me more than I can comprehend. My faith growths as I focus on him; and my doubts dissipate. It is when I distort his word or act ungraciously that I become a false witness which allows unbelief to develop as Self takes God's place. My faith is strong enough that I know in my belief he is always with me for his Love is Everlasting because he loves me!

BLESSED WORDS OF LOVE!

How sweet your words taste to me; they are sweeter than honey. (Psalm 119:103)
Your word is a lamp to guide my feet and a light for my path (Psalm 119:105)

Have you ever walked through the powerful fragrance of roses; as they sway in the wind sending wafts of perfumed spray that tickle your senses with pleasurable delight? Have you ever watched the rising sun change the gray dark dawn with orange- yellow shafts accompanied by gusts of warm air that brings life to our cool bodies? Have you ever experienced receiving wave after wave of words that feed your starved –love heart with words of sweetness that transforms your dark soul to one of "surprised joy"?

I have experienced all three. In each case they have filled me with delight but it is the sweet words that have left me with the most intense feeling of blessedness. Unlike the first two experiences which dissipate over time; sweet words fill my heart with their warmth with increasing intensity. Why is this? The first two experiences impact our external senses while words of blessings speak not only to our internal desire to be loved but they have an amazing soothing impact on the soul.

Be still before the Lord; and allow the blessings to permeate through the minutest pores of your tense soul. Like the fingers of the masseur who tenderize the knots in your muscles so these blessings will remove the knots of frustration, anger and defiance from your soul; replacing them with soothing spirits of warmth, love and affection.

Be still before the Lord; and know you are not alone. You are loved and you are blessed. You do not need to know who the messengers' maybe; or try to understand why this is happening. Just breathe in the fragrance of community love. Fill your heart with these affections of eternal blessings! Then allow the grace of God to heal the wounded scars imbedded in your heart.

Be still before the Lord; and these words of honey will transform the bitter words that lie on your lips to words of gentleness, encouragement and warmth to all you meet. For now you are no longer walking in the shadows of doubt, fear and anger; but rather in the light of God's grace and truth where agape love abides.

Be still before the Lord; so that you truly inhale the heavenly fragrance of spiritual love and wisdom. One word of blessing may change the day but an avalanche of blessing overwhelms the soul senses with such gratitude, and joy that your soul radiates the same fragrance. The once dour face shines with a thousand smiles; the sad eyes sparkle with intense mischievous sparkling light and the heart dances with the Lord's community dance of love!

With joy and laughter in my heart that is filled with gratitude for such a blessed event that opened my heart to the agape embrace I can only Bless those who have learned to acclaim and walk in the light of your presence O Lord; to rejoice in your name all day long; to exult in your righteousness. Let the aroma of Christ; the fragrance of life; and the perfume of these blessings received be ever present in my soul!

CAPSTONE OF LOVE

The stone that the builder rejected has become the capstone; the Lord has done this, and it is a marvelous in our eyes. [Psalm 118:22].

Tilling the soil that breaks the soil from its hard-crusty mass to soft broken pieces so that the rain can permeate through the soil is an edifying experience. When we encounter stones and rocks in the soil without a thought, we throw them aside. They are rejected for their perceived worthless and nuisance value. A craftsman knows his stone. He knows the right ones to use and the ones that should be rejected. The most valuable stone is the "capstone". It is the one that is placed on top of the structure and holds the structure together. Why then does the psalmist say the stone that the builder rejected has become the capstone? Simply what we see as valueless by Man has supreme value to God. Can we not also say that the capstone of our faith is Jesus the rejected stone? Jesus was rejected by mankind, he was whipped and then crucified; but on the third he rose again. This is the capstone, the highest achievement of his life. In shame and in awe, we who once rejected and now believe him can now receive salvation. We must seek forgiveness of our sins and seek sincere repentance. This will be achieved when our hearts have been transformed from one of stone to one of flesh. Our hearts are open to the word and love of God. Grace has entered our soul as in tenderizing our hearts to one of love and compassion not only to self but for others as well. The affection of love turns our eyes onto the warming light of truth, namely Jesus. We are no longer dead stone we have become living stones as Jesus Christ lives within us. In this transformation and through the teaching of the Spirit we are being rebuilt as temples of God. We are no longer valueless stones but precious jewels in the eyes of God, as we serve and preach the message of love and compassion.

COME FEED ON THE FOOD OF LOVE AND THE OIL OF JOY!

You prepare a table before me
In the presence of my enemies;
You anoint my head with oil;
My cup overflows
Psalm 23:5

Throughout my whole life a spirit of trepidation dominates my soul when invited to a feast; and for the life of me it is a puzzlement; a mystery yet unsolved. Is it I wonder because I feel a stranger at my father's house, or perhaps I am afraid to embrace the spirit of joy, or like the timid lamb I am afraid to show my real self for this would mean dropping my defences! Often at the table of the Lord I tend to be the observer, watching others rejoice because it is in this passive posture there is safety. Yet there is unrest for I sense my Lord, my shepherd is calling me to join. This meditation is an attempt to unravel this strange predicament of wanting to join the feast but choosing not to do so.

"You prepare a table" speaks of peace, hospitality; all signs of a delighted host waiting for your arrival. Care and attention to the littlest detail is given to ensure the table is fitting for the guest. This table is not just one of "bread and wine". It is one of fellowship where the shepherd embraces the lost sheep with fellowship and love. The food given is the fruit of the Spirit: love, joy, peace, patience, kindness, goodness, faithfulness, gentleness and self-control. The wonder of this table is it is prepared for YOU. It is a table so personified that your signature of hope and compassion is impressed on it. All that is wanting is the presence of the lost lamb. The shepherd can hear the beating of the lamb's heart that is so fearful and trembling before its enemies.

How indeed can there be peace when the table is set in the presence of my enemies? Be bold my lamb for do you not realize that your true enemies are what lies in the dark corner of your heart! Let go of the fears and doubts of your soul that has left you with a rigidity of immovable trembling. Look at me! Really look at me. Let our eyes look deeply into each other's eyes. Let our faces be as one. Do you not see the love, mercy and grace of your shepherd? My arms are outstretched to meet you! Come. I am here! Walk in faith to receive my love and partake at this table. Come and feed on the food of love!

As I reflect on this stand-off between the Shepherd and the lamb it is akin to the "high noon" of the sinner's salvation. If the sinner is to receive God's love there must be a confession of the spirit. The "sin" that is like a "mountainous shield" within his soul has to give way so that the light of truth can embrace his soul and the Spirit of love can heal his heart. It is indeed a step of faith that only the sinner can choose to do. None else can. This table challenges which love is to be followed: The love of darkness that leads into the valley of death or the love of truth which brings freedom, fellowship and mercy. Words of the Psalmist come to mind (Psalm 86:3-5):

Have mercy on me O Lord
For I call to you all day long
Bring joy to your servant for to you O Lord
I bring up my soul.
You are kind and forgiving O Lord
Listen to my cry of mercy
In the day of trouble, I will call you
For you will answer me

Oh, what a conundrum! Should I go to the table or not! Does he truly love me or not! Is it safe or not! The anxiety and pain of this decision is the Good Friday event of the sinner. It is where the soul must die to sin in order to be reborn on his Easter Morning. It is as this moment that both the Shepherd and the lost lamb can feel with much depth that feeling of "My God, My God, Why, hast thou forsaken me? The Shepherd compassionate cries for the possible loss of a lamb which he so loves. The Lamb pathetic bleat as the Shepherd is lost forever because of the wrong step. Imagine the joy when the darkness of the indecision is eclipsed by the light of truth as the lamb steps through the mist of salvation to embrace the Shepherd and partake of the food of life. Is it any wonder that the lamb is anointed with oil of joy and his cup of gladness overflows!

The most enigmatic aspect of this verse for me is why I find it so difficult to embrace the Lord's Table, to receive his oil of joy and live with his abundance of grace, mercy and kindness. While I am still seeking the answer. I sense the truth lies in my inability to truly relax in the Shepherd's embrace. I am still very much the tense, watchful person who has not learnt to love who I was meant to be but rather live in the sadness of what I have become. This is my burden, my mountain, my shield that holds me back from truly holding the hand of the Shepherd and allowing him to take me to the green pastures where I can rest my head and let my soul be restored.

CONFESSION IS THE GATEWAY TO FREEDOM

When you are angry, Lord, please don't punish me or correct me (v1)
I am not able to hear or speak a word; (v13)
I am completely deaf and can't make a sound (v14)
I trust you, Lord God and you will do something (v15)
I told you my sins, and I sorry for them (v18)
Stay nearby and don't desert me. (v21)
Psalm 38

There is in this sombre psalm a "suffering servant" motif. I cannot help but reflect deeply on our Saviour's last night on earth in the Garden of Gethsemane. How the Lord must have suffered in his loneliness sense of abandonment as he groped with the reality of the next day's violence and torture on his body not for anything he did that was wrong, but for who HE IS AND REPRESENTS! Our Lord and Saviour!

Lord Restore My Soul

I have read this psalm many times. It moves me! I feel the pain and anguish of the psalmist. I have walked the sheer dark abyss of isolationism where all that you can hear is your groaning and moaning. It is a place where time stands still for all is black and alien. I have learnt that physical pain and scars are temporary; while sharp at first over time they heal. What is most agonizing is the spiritual pain of mortal sin that tears your heart as efficiently as if a stiletto has stabbed your physical heart! In its path does bitterness, vengeance and hate grow if we allow it to fester. The only way to remedy this predicament is to clean and empty your heart of these dark spirits by the act of Confession. It is the gateway to Freedom. It takes courage! It needs humility! It requires faith! It grasps hope! It is letting go of self and asking your Father in heaven to help you in your time of need! It is perhaps the strongest spiritual battle I have faced.

What I am about to write is an event I have never spoken or written about before. It has sat festering in the depths of my heart for most of my life. Its impact on my life cannot be measured but it has most certainly had a profound impact on my thoughts and actions. It is a testament of God's grace and love that I have the courage to speak now! It is most fitting that this is happening in the season of Lent. My heart is being cleaned and emptied to allow the spirit of love to flow into my wanting heart!

Who has not in our lives done something wrong, which causes us to be angry and to fear the anger of the father! In my early teens my mother told me not to touch a precious china cup that was exquisite in its shape; which in adolescence defiance I did! I held it so gently in my hand it was beautiful and so delicate. "David, what did mum say!" roared my Dad. In fright I dropped the cup. It broke in a thousand pieces. In fright I ran with the echo of my father's voice following I ran through the streets, over the bridge, over the fields, scratching my legs from blackberry thorns. I slipped on some mud bruising my face and hands. Finally, with tears rolling down my face I looked miserably at the rolling waves of the Atlantic Channel as I sat on a flat rock on the Tor of the cliff. Normally this was a beauty and peaceful sight. Today all was gray, menacing and accusing. I knew I had done wrong! I knew I was in trouble! I was too afraid to go back and face the "music". My body hurt! My muscles ached! I closed my eyes searching for a peace that would not come. "There you are, Brat! Are you so much of a coward you cannot face me" With this accusation my father lifted me up and threw me over his lap, tore my pants to my ankle and proceeded to spank me with his walking cane. My lips remained tightly closed in defiant surrender. With a beating heart did I endure the pain, the humiliation and the surging rage within me! When it was over and my father's retribution was sated; he told me to dress and follow him home. In silence did we return to a place that did not feel like home! He was in front and me behind him with a bowed head. What a sad puppy I was! How my body ached; I could feel the blood dripping down my legs from my bruised battered butt. Every leaden step sent shudders of pain through me. How at that moment did I feel hate for my father; such was the rage within me that father in a very sense was dead in my heart! I was deaf and dumb to any word he said to me! I was alone! I felt deeply unloved! I ached for companionship! From that day I said very few words to him. I kept a stony silence bred by bitterness and anger!

Some months later when lying in bed in a dark mood I cried out "Lord if you there! If you care for me DO SOMETHING! Then I in desperation confessed my unloving rebellious behaviour and finished off the prayer with a quick I trust you Lord! Inexplicably a spirit of peace swept through me; where there was once darkness and despair emerged a feeling of warmth and a hope. I slept well that night' a joy from many months of nights where I tossed and turned. In a spirit of hope I thank the Lord and urge Him never to abandon me. Little did I know this was the beginning of a long journey searching for a love that was lost!

Six decades have passed since this instance. He has never left me. Yes, I still have my dark moments but these are testing times. He is emptying my heart from fear, darkness and despair. My heart while still scarred I believe has become more tender and loving. This path of freedom in my life started when I confessed and chose my Lord to be my "Abba Father". I am glad I did (actually with his help).

You are the Lord God. Stay close and don't desert me. You are the one who saves me.

CONTENTMENT OF THE HEART IS THE FIBRE OF FAITH

Wait for the Lord; be strong and take heart and wait for the Lord – Psalm 27:14
I have learned to be content, in whatever the circumstances – Philippians 4:11

There were two mountaineers both seeking to climb to the rugged point of the summit. Each is well supplied with all the mountain gear, rope and clamps. They were both equally determined to climb. One of the climbers was not happy with equipment and appeared to have concern about the safety strength of his clamps and rope. No one could satisfy him! What was surprising the other climber had the identical equipment, and he had no complaints. In fact, he had faith in his equipment. There was an inner strength of contentment about his aura that suggested all will be well!

In the quiet of the sanctuary I sat pondering on the question this scenario suggested: Why is it that some people become agitated and dissatisfied while others over the same concerns are calm and collective. More particularly can a person of faith be contented? What about a church whose congregation is discontent? Psalm 27 is a declaration of faith for it begins with the Lord is my light and salvation! The Psalmist vividly shows that with all his human weaknesses he is a Man of God who dearly loves his Lord! He has a passion to do Gods' work, to be his obedient Servant. He is discontent when he fails. His heart for ever seeks the Lord. He sees God as His light and His salvation! He is not afraid for God is his strength! He is confident for God is His protector. His gazes on the beauty of the Lord! He knows while friends and family will forsake him, God will never leave him! Even when he fails his God! This is why even in the moods of discontent and in the spirit of darkness, his heart is content to wait for the Lord, for God is Good and is his Strength!

What I discern is that if the fibre of my faith is strong and firm then any discomfort, dissatisfaction or disappointment I may have about myself and what others may be doing may cause me distress' but my heart will be content in the knowledge that the Lord abides in me! It is when my heart is fickle and my faith weak that the discontent of anxiety within my heart closes the door on God's mercy and grace. This is why I see contentment as the fibre of faith. This in turn raises the question how do you ascertain this strength of faith?

Paul in Philippians writes: I have learnt the secret of being content in any and every situation, whether we feel well fed or hungry; whether living in plenty or in want. I can do everything through him who gives me strength. (Philippians 4:12-13) This strength comes from a spirit of humility and gentleness that has its grounding in God's love. Let your gentleness be evident to all. The Lord is near. Do not be anxious about anything, but in everything, by prayer and petition, with thanksgiving, present your requests to the Lord. Philippians 4:5-6)

The inner strength of the Christian Church is to be a prayerful church that displays its confident, calmness and contentment by its actions, because they have the deep, deep knowledge that God is with them and will never be abandoned. It is this strong fibre of faith that sustains the Church during adversity and confrontations. The church must help and guard its parishioners from having a spirit of discontent that comes from the dark forces of doubt, angst and disbelief, which can produce a spirit of little faith that leads to a discontentment where the fibres of faith are broken and weak! It behoves the church to be ever watchful and vigilant to discern the root of the discontent. To know whether the discontent comes from a fickle heart or from a faithful heart that desires God's Kingdom of Heaven on earth will vitally impact the Church's mission focus.

If there is one thing I desire the most is to live in a restful, serene place; for far too long my spirit has been one long continuum of ups and downs, with more times of angst and insecurities with few times of joyful delight! How, I long to truly shout with joy, singing and praising delighting in the His presence

Lord Restore My Soul

but for unfathomable reasons, Lord I find my voice is muted as if I am too afraid to let go! This Lord is the crux of the matter! I am far too sensitive for my own good. I have lived in the shadows out of fear of authority's sting where love was missing. Avoidance has become my guardian; thus, preventing the warm spirit of love to sooth my soul. I confess Lord, I distrust love with a passion. It is best to say nothing. Let the hurt in my heart remain for to receive another rejected love will be too much to bear! In my solitary journey I am wary to open the door to love. Paradoxically in this state I hear your whisper and like the psalmist I hear the Lord say "come and talk with me. When my heart pains for love I respond, Lord, I am coming! When pride, rebellion and defiance stalk my heart I walk my path alone refusing to obey the whisper. But your patience Lord is eternal! I know if my heart accepts the deep, deep love of your grace my contentment will strengthen the fibre of my faith.

With numbing truth does the psalmist not only express the condition of his soul but with stunning sharpness does he express my heart's anxiety:

Do not turn your back on me.
Do not reject your servant in anger.
You have always been my helper.
Don't leave me now; don't abandon me.
O God of my salvation!
Even if my father and mother abandon me,
The Lord will hold me close.

The path of abandonment is ever before me! I hate it! I despise it! I even curse it! From birth to adolescence the spirit of abandonment has been my constant companion! It has scarred my heart. Yet Lord I am weary of walking in the shadows. It is time for me to walk the path of light; the way of salvation! Lord, to be held close is alien and fearful to me. Be merciful and answer me!

Above all it is my prayer that my heart will be open to your compassion and love. Teach me how to live, O Lord. Lead me along the right path.... Let me see your goodness and let my will be patient, courageous and strong.

Let my trust in you Lord be such that my love for you is unfailing; let my heart learn how to shout with joy when you have healed my heart; let the love in my heart pour out compassion and grace to all I meet; and let me Lord love you with unbounding tears of joy. This is my prayer! This is my path of light and salvation I wish to walk! Come Lord! Walk beside me! Let us talk and rejoice!

This is my prayer for the Church that it will not leave its spirit of faith because of the forces of darkness, violence and unrest. May your peace and your joy guide us to the place where we can wait for You Lord with the assurance you will never abandon us. Let us not abandon you!

LORD RESTORE MY SOUL

HE CREATED EVERYTHING AND IT WAS GOOD!

DARK NIGHT BECOMES DAWN OF LOVE

It was a beautiful blue and sunny day as I sat on the boat of hope in the sea of love and delight. The water was clear, calm and sparkling. Its very presence gave me peace and refreshed my spirit. The warm breeze was balm to my soul and soothed my tense muscles, allowing me to relax and enjoy the presence of the moment. The flow of faith guided me through the waters of assurance for I was entering the door to my spiritual home. I was about to meet the one I loved with all my heart. A place I have long journeyed to find. I lay back both with contentment and excitement. My heart beat with ever eager pulse as I approached the source of my love. When without warning dark rolling clouds of doubt flowed overhead turning the brightness to a menacing grey. Sprays of discontent cooled my soul. Rough waters produced a wandering love as waves battered the boat. Mists of confusion enveloped the boat; to the point nothing could be seen! Where I was going; I did not know. Nothing could be heard. I shouted for help! No response came! A fear of incredible feroc-

Lord Restore My Soul

ity hit my soul as a sense of abandonment pierced my heart. Mocking cries of unworthiness tore the unity of love in my spirit to threads. Shreds of icy thoughts struck me that I was no longer blessed. A pain beyond pain embedded itself into the innermost chambers of my heart! My spiritual home was perhaps a mere fantasy! I was left to drift in the endless sea of doubt and despair. I felt miserable and very much alone! Words of prayer failed me! Expressions of adoration and awe to my savour were no more. All I can do is cry with dry tears for God's mercy to protect my soul. I felt my beloved had deserted me- the dark night of my soul had entered my heart. The spirit of desolation and a sense of nothingness ran rampant through my soul. I sought the refreshing waters of hope but the cup was dry. All I had left was a hope beyond reason that God was still with me. The pain within me was nothing to the pain of love lost! Once more my heart felt homeless, lonely and full of despair! With Angst I looked and all I could see was a thimble of light in the distance; a shard of faith illuminating the dense nothingness.

Be kind to me, God-
I'm in deep trouble again.
I've cried my eyes out;
I feel hollow inside.
My life leaks away, groan by groan;
My years fade out in sighs. [Psalm 31:9-10]

Open up before God, keep nothing back,
He'll do whatever needs to be done:

*He'll validate your life in the clear light of day
And stamp you with approval at high noon.
Quiet down before God, be prayerful before
Him. [Psalm 37:5-7]*

*Why am I so discouraged?
Why is my heart so sad?
I will put my hope in God!
I will praise Him again – My saviour and my
God! [Psalm 42:11]*

Just as the year has its seasons; so, do I have my spiritual seasons; but what does remain eternal is my faith in God. My walk can be close to his heart which leaves me in a spirit of joy. There are times when my spirit is dry for, I know not what to say and all I can do is remain silent and listen for his return. Then there have been a few times my soul has been so much in despair that I feel chain bound in my dark spirit of nothingness; isolated from all things; where even the presence of God has vanished. All I have been left with is the memory of love lost. In this state I hold onto this shred of love with the utmost passion; for I know this love is the light that will guide me to the place where he is waiting for me.

The darkness of my soul only sees this light as a pinprick of hope; in the place where my soul is constantly tormented, by teasing clouds of doubt and mocking gusts of hysteria that seem to shred my faith with unwanted pain and fear. While this state has deep psychological negative impact on my emotions, where I withdraw and become gloomier in outlook; this is only a consequence of my spiritual battle that lies within. It is here the cry of Jesus comes most profoundly to me "Why have you forsaken me, O Lord?" In puzzlement and confusion, I cry "Why Lord have you hidden yourself?" But all is silent. I am in no position to hear the soothing words of my Lord. All I can do is sit and pray for his compassionate mercy.

I know I am entering a dangerous phase of my spiritual journey that cannot be explained through human communication. Even now my understanding of the spiritual world is in its total infancy where cognitive understanding is vague and incomprehensible. What I comprehend is that my heart of love faces the spiritual battle that lies between darkness and light, between hope and despair, and between fear and love. My heart has reached a point of cleansing that must occur if I am to continue my journey towards my spiritual home resting in the glory of God's love. I am at that critical point of will I let go of my "dark angels of doubt, fear and distrust" and open my heart in total vulnerability to the angels of God's love "mercy, grace and compassion". Here in this unfolding struggle I will discover the extent darkness holds on me and the depth of my passionate love for my Lord! Lord in my haste to solve this dilemma I pray that I do not fall helter-skelter into the spirit of Acedia where apathy and indifference reigns! May I ever be alert as to why I am in this darkness of spirit! It is to purify me from my sins.

Create in me a heart that has been emptied of human arrogance so that now in humility I can receive the pure love of God!

DEEP ROOTS OF GOD'S LOVE

The Lord does not look at the things man looks at. Man looks at the outward appearance but the Lord looks at the inner heart. [1 Samuel 16:7]. The Lord is with me; I will not be afraid. What can man do to me? The Lord is my helper. It is better to take refuge in the Lord than to trust in man. [Psalm 118:6-8]. God did not give us a spirit of timidity but a spirit of power, of love and of self-discipline. [2 Timothy 1:7].

The longer I live; the shorter I realize my life is. Our time on this earth is so tenuous. There is a desire to make the most of our life, to have the respect of others, to perhaps leave a legacy and to continue the name of family. Words of affirmation, encouragement and praise tenderize our battered soul. There is nothing worse than feeling isolated, adrift and unwanted in the vast wilderness of society. Have you noticed how deep the tree roots are in a healthy forest? So, it is with us the deeper our roots are with others the more stable is our view of life. The tentacles of relationships, the bonds of family and warmth of friendship all provide identity and position. Of all our relationships the most crucial and often taken for granted is the one with our God. If you are like me, I have never been comfortable when a medical specialist examines my body; there is an intrusion which is cold and indifferent. It is as if part of my private life is now public but I know it is for my good that this intrusion takes place. So, it is with God, we must let him enter the most private and vulnerable area of our soul; that is our heart! Perhaps our fears are simply because we do not trust our heart or we just do not want God to know who we really are. We therefore out of choice live in fear and reject the hand of God to heal the wounded heart. We thus turn our back on our Creator, the one who is the Comforter and our Savior. Why do we do this?

Our pride and arrogance is part of the answer; the other part is we can have a deep fear of love. The kiss of friendship can be more frightening than the fist of man. In the latter our defenses are up but in the former our vulnerability is at its most extreme. In that loving friendship our attitude is one of total submission and one of absolute trust. Lord, I am yours; do to me, what you will; I will obey. It is an obedience rooted in love and compassion; there is no force or coercion. It is an act that results from the spirit of grace that has entered our hearts and has empowered us to be what God intended. By allowing God to enter the refuge of our heart, we have also entered the refuge of God's home. As he, through his warm embrace and loving touch, repairs the wounds; we learn to love and accept ourselves more and are able to love and accept others. We know we are beloved and blessed! We do not need the endorsement of others; but now overpowered by God's love where the cup overflows with his grace; we can pass this love onto others. Only when we reach this spiritual maturity do we understand that God did not give us a spirit of timidity but a spirit of power, of love and of self-discipline.

Our first step is to turn our eyes to our Lord and in the stillness of the moment sit calmly and wait for the presence of the Lord to enter our hearts. Initially there will be resistance until mind and body just focuses on the Lord and then he will come and you will feel the tenderness of his touch and the whisper of his love. In the paralysis of that moment all is still in the presence of love! What is wounded is healed! Where there was anxiety is now peace! Where there was anger is now adoration! There is nothing you can do but bask the warmth of his grace and be empowered by his compassion. Such is the love of God and the fickleness of man! In him we have a friend and companion for life. We are truly blessed and loved!

DELIGHT YOURSELF IN THE AWE OF GOD'S CREATION

My soul thirsts for you, my body longs for you in a dry and weary land where there is no water [Psalm 63:1].

I remember too well those days when I hiked in the mountains, when my body received the refreshing cold water that re-energized my body to continue on my journey. I was often tired and my body ached but the sheer joy of achievement accomplished always motivated me to finish. So it was with the spirit of ardor, determination and tenacity that I went on these hikes. There is something uniquely special walking in the splendor and majesty of nature. You realize how insignificant you are when faced with nature's challenges. You are in awe at the diversity of color and shape of nature's design. There is for me something extremely mystical watching the cumulous billowing clouds float silently through the blue sky casting shadows of coolness on the dry land below. Who has not looked in wonder at nature's tapestry from the perch on a mountain's summit? It is at these sacred moments you know this world is no accident; it is too wondrously made. Your soul turns in gratitude to your creator. When our soul is tired, weary and dry from spiritual struggles do we still seek God or do we turn to our own resources. At these testing times do we still trust God and remain firm in our faith. Or do we become like the lost sheep living in our own pastures of doubt, anger and despair. It is easier to follow God, our shepherd in the "good" times; but it is when life "struggles" over power us that the love of God and the guiding hand of the shepherd are most needed. In our dark moments is our faith strong enough to still delight in the Lord and to allow him to give the desires of our heart and in so doing we will receive the refreshing spiritual waters that quench our dry soul. As the psalmist says all we have to do is: Trust in the Lord and do good. Believe in God, believe in yourself and above all love your neighbor as God has loved you so that you can truly love yourself.

DESIRE FOR GOD'S JOY

But may the righteous be glad and rejoice before the Lord may they be happy and joyful. Sing to God, praise his name, extol him who rides on the cloud – his name is the Lord – and rejoice before him [Psalm 68:3-4]. Yet O Lord you are my Father. We are the clay. You are the potter. We are the work of your hand. [Isaiah 64:8]. He will turn the hearts of the fathers to their children and the hearts of the children to their fathers. [Malachi 4:6ff].

What prevents a person from rejoicing? Is it the loss of spontaneity? Is it a failure to appreciate the wonder of the inexplicable? Or is it the inability to feel free to relax? Or just that a spirit of sadness that pervades the soul? All of the above are present and at times can prevent the sheer delight of living God's grace and joy. C.S. Lewis called this "surprised by joy".

It is a spontaneous reaction that pleases the soul, brings sparkles to the eyes and a smile to the lips. You cannot pre-plan joy; it takes you unawares in a wonderful relaxing way. It makes you want to sing and to speak in love and adoration. We are wired differently, some of us are passive, others are active;

many are introverts while others are extroverts; but what is common we are the "work of God's hands". If we will let him, he will turn our hearts to his love and grace. We need to have a heart that is receptive. If our soul is burdened and troubled it is difficult to see joy because of the fog of despair. This can be achieved if we are willing to be disciplined and look to the Holy Spirit to teach us. Firstly, we need to be in a state of "Being" that is to be still and listening to the word of God. As we do, we notice more deeply our surroundings and discern the inner condition of our heart. Secondly, we need to "Breathe" more slowly and smell the aroma around us and the sweet aroma of God's word. As we perfect this breathing we will come to delight in the sweetness and the touch of God's love and soothing spirit of grace. Thirdly, we must truly "Believe" that God's word is true and that through our actions of prayer, reading and charity we will learn not to doubt but to soak in his word as the bread of life. Fourthly, we must know we "Belong" to God's community. We are not alone, for to appreciate the depth and breadth of God's compassion and love will only occur as we participate in community. As we discipline ourselves darkness, despair, and despondency will leave the soul as the light of joy, gladness and rejoicing slips into the vacuum. Our hearts are full of God's grace and with awesome wonder we praise his name!

DO NOT BE ANGRY; SEEK GOD'S LOVE

"Do not be angry beyond measure Lord; do not remember our sins forever. [Isaiah 64:9]. How long will your anger smolder against the prayers of your people? [Psalm 80:4] I will praise you, O Lord. Although you were angry with me, your anger turned away and you have comforted me. [Isaiah 12:1] Do not let the sun go down while you are angry. [Ephesians 4:26]. This is how we know that we love the children of God: by loving God and carrying out his commands. [1 John 5:2]. Christ did not receive the spirit for himself but rather for us in him, for it is also through Christ that all gifts come down to us [St Cyril of Alexandria].

At first it seems strange and out of character to us for God to be angry. After all, God is love! Think for a moment, how many of us have seen our parents angry at us. If we think further there was a good reason. They love us, they care for us and when we disappoint or commit an act that can hurt us and them, they are justifiably upset. In fact, if no anger was displayed when such an act occurred, we might wonder whether they care about us at all.

The psalmist knows he has sinned and cries for God mercy not to be "over measure". In his love for God, he fears the wrath of God. Do we truly fear God or simply take him for granted? The depths of our love for God will be a measure of our fear of God. We know anger can be destructive, violent and hateful. This is an emotion not of love but of pride. Its source is sin and its goal is vengeance, or to hurt, or to humiliate. It is born out of fear not out of love. It comes from a wound deep in the heart and it is a defense reflex to insulate this wound of anxiety, or lack of self-worth. The only cure for this anger is to remove what ails us and by seeking help, repenting and asking for forgiveness from God. But it can also be an emotion derived from fear of losing one who we love because of their wanton act or by a violent act of another!

To allow our heart to receive the Spirit of compassion and of love from our Savior Jesus Christ; our hearts must be open, be free and be vulnerable. This is why we must take the time to confess our troubles before the "end of the day" so that the wound does not fester in our hearts as we sleep. If we do not do this, we allow the spirit of love to dissipate and the seeds of bitterness and disunity to dominate our thoughts and when we wake up our soul will be dark and full of anger. We want the "breath of the Lord to breathe on us" so that we receive the warm loving spirit of God. Let us remember that God's love is born out of compassion and love for us. It is born from his goodness for this is his essence. We can praise him with certainty that his care is eternal. We know we have the love of God in us when we share God's spirit, through us, with others. God's love is not selfish, it is unconditional love. Let us take heed when those we love are angry at us. It is an act of love! Let us seek discernment. And then let us praise and be thankful for such a friend, for such a God.

EMOTIONS ARE A BEACON TO OUR SOUL

I am worn out from groaning; all day long I flood my bed with weeping and drench my couch with tears [Psalm 6:6]. Not a word from their mouth can be trusted; their heart is filled with destruction. Their throat is an open grave; with their tongue they speak deceit [Psalm 5:9] To fear the Lord is the root of wisdom and her branches are long life –[Ecclesiastics 1:25]. Jesus said," Come follow me and I will make you fishers of men". At once they left their nets and followed him [Mark 1:17-18]

Our emotions are a beacon to our soul. Our actions signify our beliefs. Who has not had those times when the soul is troubled as a consequence of what we have done or what others have done or might do to us?

Death of a close relative and friend produces the most turbulent and violent emotions within us. It is an honest reaction to a permanent fracture in a close friendship. Part of us dies with this loss, for a love has been extinguished. This emotion can also arise from fear of retribution; where we have committed a wrong and fear vengeance and judgment from the wounded party. We are solely afraid. In our darkness, God is absent in our heart. In this condition we are extremely vulnerable. We can repent of our sins to God and open our hearts to healing. Or we can close our souls to his redeeming love and justify what has occurred through lies and false rationalization. We continue to live in fear of others and ourselves. Addiction to sin becomes a refuge instead of seeking God's refuge.

Over time we lose the passion in our heart and we become emotionally inert and spiritually neutral to our fallen condition. Apathy and passivity dominate our thoughts and actions. In a sense we are like the walking "dead". We are own enemy, imprisoned by our own actions. Nothing will change until we recognize and start to fear God. Fear is the flip side of love; if we have no love, we have no fear. This is why "to fear the Lord is the root of wisdom". When we are in a loving relationship, we will do everything to keep it; for we fear the vacuum, the emptiness when love is absent. It is the absence of God, the withholding of his love that we wish to avoid. The recognition of this fact is the first step to repentance and reconciliation. As we open our hearts to his voice and to his love; we are more open to accepting his call.

When he says "come, follow me" we are more likely to respond in affirmative obedience. Mark says so much in a few words, when Simon and Andrew drop their nets to follow Christ. Was it the words of Christ? Was it his character? Or was it, Christ's very presence that persuaded them to give everything up to follow Christ. How many of us would do the same? Are we just as trusting as Andrew and Peter? To me this is the mark of true faith, to say yes to a way of life which you have no understanding where it will lead. All you have is a belief in the leader who calls you. This is passionate obedience. This is a true act of faith. The small seed of faith was dropped on the ground; they accepted the seed and they became giants in their faith. – "her branches are long life"

FACE OF LOVE

The Lord said "You cannot see my face for no one may see my face and l live." I have sought your face with all my heart [Psalm 119.58]. We are who with unveiled faces are reflecting the Lord's Glory [2 Corinthians 3:18].

Why is the face so important? Why is it some people avoid looking at the face? And others seek it with joy? Why indeed does the Lord say we cannot see his face!

The face is the organ of emotions of our soul; just as the eyes are the windows of our heart. The face is the most powerful channel of nonverbal communication; just as our prayers are the most potent channel of intercession with our Lord.

A tense face suggests inward struggles. A happy face with a radiant smile brings peace to all they meet. Without a word spoken we so often make discernment about a person by facial expression. But I wonder if this is truly fair; for while the face expresses emotion, all that is being reflected is the experiences of past life; what we hope for the future or how we see the present. What is being expressed may show a false reflection of who we really are. When we look at ourselves in a mirror; who do we see? Do we only see what we want to see instead of what we ought to see? And what applies to us; will also apply to how we reflect our views on others which predetermines how we show love to others and even ourselves.

The other day I re-read this poem, author unknown, called the Mask:

I keep my mask with me everywhere I go
In case I need to wear it, it doesn't show
I'm so afraid to show you ME, afraid of what you'll do
You might laugh at ME, or say mean things
Or I might lose you.
I'd like to take my mask off, to let you look at ME
I want you to try to understand.
And please love what you see.
So, if you'll be patient and close your eyes
I'll pull it off real slow
Please understand how much it hurts
To let the real ME show
Now my mask is taken off. I feel naked! Bare! So cold!
If you can still love all you see
You're my friend, pure as gold.
I want to save my mask and hold it in my hand
I need to keep handy if someone doesn't understand

Please protect ME my new friend, thank you for loving ME true, But please let me keep my mask with me, until I love ME too.

Can you not sense the low esteem, the loneliness, and the search for love that permeates this poem? It is such fear that forces the mask of deception to hide the hurts and the wounds. Unless corrected we are doomed to live in a New Orleans masked dance of false jollity. Thus, caught in our own fantasies of fear and trembling where the real face loses significance as the mask of unreality overcomes!

Kierkegaard in his prayer Thou hearest our cry wrote if the forgotten one has separated himself from all others; thou knowest him. Kierkegaard knew loneliness; he knew what it meant to be scorned and ridiculed; but he never forgot even in his most dark times that God was always with him. It takes much faith to believe in the presence of God when you walk in the valley of darkness; for God seems distant and absent. David in his psalms sought the face of God for comfort, for guidance and for joy. Moses was so close to God he wanted to see God's face which is a natural for friends to desire; but God warned that this was impossible to do so would mean Moses' would die. The reflection of God's light is too strong for our eyes! The brilliance of divinity is so pure and so mystical it is more than our mortal eyes can bear!

To me the wonderful news is we are made in God's image and our faces should reflect the Lord's glory. The greater our faith the more powerful is God reflected in our face. The more we walk in the light of God and bask in God's mercy; the more will the radiance of our faith shine in our face!

The question is then how does one who walks in darkness and wears his mask of deception able to find God's face? By desiring to open his heart to God's love and by listening to God's word. Only through a change of heart will the face change; for what our externalities show are simply a reflection of the internal state of our soul.

This change cannot be done alone. It needs the help of a friend, a hand of compassion, a touch of love, and a word of assurance. But all of these come second to the radiant face that provides the connection of warmth and reassurance. It is the face that bestows trust, respect, understanding and love to the one that seeks God's glory! It is the face that exemplifies Our Lord Jesus mission to save sinners and says come "Follow Me". It is the face that is non-judgmental, gentle and patient. It is the face that tenderly removes the mask from the wounded face so that God's light can massage the face with the tender warm love of Gods' grace.

We are to mirror Christ's love to the world through our own sacrifices and devotions! Let our face truly reflect God's love in all we say and do.

Show me your face; let me hear your voice!
For your voice is sweet
And your face is lovely   [Song of Songs 2:14]

FORGIVENESS IS THE KEY TO GOD'S HEART!

*1 Our God, you bless everyone
   whose sins you forgive and wipe away.
2 You bless them by saying,
   "You told me your sins, without trying to hide them, and now I forgive you."
3 Before I confessed my sins, my bones felt limp,
   and I groaned all day long.
4 Night and day your hand weighed heavily on me, and my strength was gone as in the summer heat.
5 So I confessed my sins and told them all to you. I said, "I'll tell the LORD each one of my sins." Then you forgave me and took away my guilt. Psalm 32:1--5*

Contemplation of this Psalm must also include the contemplation of Jesus' words on the cross: Father, forgive them, for they do not know what they are doing" Luke 23:34. It is a shocking fact and a terrible indictment on humanity that our Lord while in utter pain on the cross still had the love and compassion to ask his Father to forgive. To forgive the false accusers of their crimes which led Him to the cross. With this statement Jesus in his last breaths was expressing his love for God's people with his incredible love for His Father. It is a wonderful testimony on God's incredible grace and mercy!

Yet how many times have I gone to the altar with a spirit of anger and frustration because of a hurt, a broken promise, a wrong word and a betrayed love. I weep inwardly at the times I have confessed my failures with my mouth but my heart is still in defiance. My soul is indeed heavy and my spirit dries up. The bread and wine do not fill me with joy!

What is worse I know I should not have gone but felt compelled to do so. Why? The spirit of darkness was struggling with the spirit of love. The compassion of my God was calling me to come but the dark spirit of self-pity was preventing its joy to enter my heart. My heart was not pure before God. My spirit of unforgiveness is indeed a barrier to reconciliation before God. The rebel within my heart needed to become a lamb of God. In such a condition there is no way I could ever receive God's blessings.

How well I know the very thought confession does cause my bones to feel limp, and I groan all day long, I know when I have sinned and the curse of pride brings defiance into my heart. I falter because I fear the forgiveness will not be granted and acknowledging the sin will expose even more my sense of unworthiness.

Oh, if I could only imprint in my heart that the

act of forgiveness comes from the spirit of love and grace. It can never come from a dark spirit of hate. Forgiveness is the key to God. It is the unlocking of the door that binds you in sin. It allows guilt to fly out and the fragrance of love to come into your heart. It replaces the dark spirit of remorse with the enlightened spirit of joy. No longer are you alone bound as a prisoner with your sin; you become free to love, to serve and to bring joy to others. Forgiveness has not only freed your soul you have also been blessed for God is well pleased with you" May this promise remain embedded in my heart so that I might adore and serve my Lord!

FRAGRANT LOVE RESPONDS TO THE CALL OF LOVE

You did not choose me but you to go and bear fruit – fruit that will last. Then the Father will give you whatever you ask in my name. This is my command: Love each other. (John 15: 16-17)
My lover is mine and I am his. (Song of Songs 3:16)
When your words came I ate them; they were my joy and my heart's delight. (Jeremiah 15:16)
Be imitators of God, therefore, as dearly loved children, and live a life of love just as Christ loved us and gave himself up for us a fragrant offering and a sacrifice to God. (Ephesians 5:1-2)

To call Jesus words to his disciples the Sermon of the Mount to me is unfortunate; for it is more of a homily of how to nurture your heart in the spirit of fragrant grace!

It was very much an intimate group that sat before their Rabbi in the solitude of the mountain top. It is a fitting place for it is here at the peak of the summit where the spirit of love soars serenely through the souls and heart of seekers of God's truth. Here Jesus faced his chosen leaders who he loved most deeply; and it is in this spirit of desire and warmth he expresses how this love can be communicated, nurtured and sustained.

There is a profound truth! If my heart does not seek God's love or even accepts his love with the wonder and intense grace where my spirit of love has not intertwined with the love of Christ's love for me; then the depth and essence of what Jesus expressed in this homily will be sorely missed. In the shallowness of such love the homily become more like philosophical legalistic principles rather than nuggets of love expressions.

How Blessed we are when we experience within our heart that love for another which takes our breath away in wonder and causes our heart to beat in faster rhythm just to see, to feel and to serve our beloved. How our spirit soars with joy and delight in the presence of the beloved. How we humble ourselves before such majestic beauty. How we prostrate ourselves to protect, to follow and to obey the very wishes of the one we love. How free is our spirit when we can freely give all we love in the spirit of loving grace!

How Blessed we are when we can in this spirit of love empathize, comfort and mourn with those we love who are in pain, in distress and are in need of encouragement. In such love there is no loneliness only the embrace of fellowship, the word of hope and the touch of kindness as we love our neighbour!

How Blessed we are when our heart is centered on serving our beloved with humility and kindness instead of the spirit of accumulation and lordship where power, pride and prejudice reigns. Love is indeed gentle and understanding. It is the spirit of unity rather than divisiveness. It is the spirit of understanding rather than confusion. It is the spirit that inherits the dispossessed to a place of warm nurturing community where understanding, Charis and love sparks with joyful life!

How Blessed we are when our heart is filled with the deep, deep love of our beloved that gives us strength and insight to treat all we meet with the same spirit of grace, equality, equity regardless of their position in the community. In this thirst to satisfy our beloved we also have the same thirst to help our community. In this mutual love of respect, grace and compassion will the sins of injustice be eliminated and all "ism" will be erased before the spirit of agape love.

How Blessed we are when our hearts are full of overwhelming compassion for the sacrificial love of our beloved that leads us to be compassionate in our actions to the suffering, to the persecuted, to the unloved of our world for we in turn will receive mercy. Kindness in love ignites an uncaring community to one of caring and loving for neighbour.

How blessed we are when our hearts are truly open and vulnerable to our beloved for nothing will be hidden; our soul will be intertwined with the soul of our beloved into that realm of united bliss where the breath of our life walks with automatic rhythm with the love of our heart! Oh, with such love it will be walking the air of purity, insight and companionship with our beloved!

How blessed we are when we live in the fragrance of that love of peace and joy, where words are like sweet nectar flowing from our lips and our breath bring such soothing music to our ears. In such a spirit frictions, discontent, tempers and discord exist with such rarity for agape love flowers with colourful abandon because unity of loving peace reigns supreme.

How blessed we are when this love is strong in conviction and intensely felt in our hearts that no word or action can take it away. It is simply a sacrificial love that is beyond human reasoning. It is sacred love where two hearts have become united with one. It is a love that has been soaked with the divine oil of joy that nothing breaks asunder. It is a love that is sealed: we have been chosen, accepted and called!

We are truly blessed for our heart is one with our Saviour! In this love he calls us to Love our Neighbour and if we do this the fragrance of his love will be with us now, forever and eternally!

We are called to love. Let us harken to this love. Smell and receive the fragrant joy of his eternal blessing

How Blessed we are to know that God has anointed us with the oil of joy. (Psalm 45:7) because of faithful love to Him.

FREEING BREATH OF JOY

He breathed into his nostrils the breath of life, and man became a living being. (Genesis 2:7) And with that he breathed on them and said, "Receive the Holy Spirit" (John 20:22). Each Man's life is but a breath. (Psalm 39:5ff). He himself gives all men life and breath and everything else [Acts 17:24 ff]

It is a constant joy of serenity and peace to walk barefoot on a soft sandy golden beach feeling the gentle warming sea breeze encircle my body like some cleansing agent and the soft sand sifting between my toes. I can feel the tension of life loosening its grip as the soothing fingers of the breeze massage my soul. With sheer delight I watch the sparkling white crests of wavelets, shining with diamond glitter in the glow of the early morning sun, sweep majestically over the sand bringing new life in its water apron and then with a musical swish retreating cleaning all that has been covered. If I look carefully I see the little crabs digging feverishly to hide themselves in the sand before the swooping sandpipers discover their existence and before the waves once more cover the sand and then to retreat again. The beach sounds are constant whether they are the swirling music of the waves or the sad notes of the Seagulls or the shrill of the cormorants or the shrill of the sandpipers; they are all wondrous music of joy to my ears. In this cacophony of sound and colour time becomes timeless. All I can do is breathe in the glory of God's creation and breathe out the tensions of life.

As I soak in this scene I am in awe of the majestic nature that has been created, that has been here before my time and will remain here well after I have left. There is permanency in knowing that the ebbs and flow of nature is eternal and that the ups and downs of my life are temporary. True security is not in my nostalgic past or in the fear of what tomorrow might bring but living the in present and glorifying the moment the Lord has given me! With this knowledge I find I can breathe more calmly, more in awe and more sedately as I enjoy just being in His presence!

Let us then admire the shells on the beach as we climb out of our own shells of darkness, trepidations and anxieties. Let us look in wonder at the breadth and the variety of the wonders of God's creation so that we can breathe in their scent and perfume that refreshes and energises our souls. Let us with full abandon breathe in the beauty, the power and the warmth of God's presence as we unfetter the chains of bondage that torment our souls. Let us bask in the warmth of the Sun and with welcoming lips kiss the breath of life so the Great Comforter can abide in our heart. Let our life exemplify the final words of the psalmist: "Let everything that has breath praise the Lord".

Breathe on me, breath of God,
Fill me with life anew,
That I may love what Thou dost love,
And do what Thou wouldst do.
Breathe on me, breath of God,
Until my heart is pure,
Until with Thee I will one will,
To do and to endure.
Breathe on me, breath of God,
Blend all my soul with Thine,
Until this earthly part of me
Glows with Thy fire divine.
Breathe on me, breath of God,
So shall I never die,
But live with Thee the perfect life
Of Thine eternity.

Words by Edwin Hatch 1878

GLORIOUS THINGS ARE SAID OF YOU

Glorious things are said of you – Psalm 87:3
Being strengthened with all the power according to his glorious might so
That you may have great endurance and patience
And joyfully giving thanks to the Father- Colossians 1:11ff

There are 44 verses in the Bible referring to glory and glorious which is a study in itself. What intrigues me in this mediation is how we understand and use it today. We talk about a glorious sunset! We rarely say it was a glorious win; but rather we use a synonym like magnificent win. We may say it is a glorious dress; but how often do we say that person is glorious. What strikes me about how we use "Glorious" is to describe earthly things rather than divine attributes.

It is very striking that in Psalm 87 that the Creator our Lord says the people in the city of God are "Glorious" not because of their appearance but rather what they have done. God loved this city. It is his elect city. This is the magnificent worthy city of Jerusalem. His temple resided in this city. It is a city that demands respect, honour and majesty. The splendour of the city evoked feelings of admiration, delight and joy. This city worshipped their God! This city is and always will be a special city!

When I survey the incredible colour display of the dawn; or the awesome vista of the valley diverse colours and shapes; or the immensity and awesome power of nature the word "glorious" sits on my lips as I whisper in wonder God's magnificence power and majesty. In these moments I am very conscious of my insignificance before these powers of beauty! I struggle why such a powerful glorious God would take notice of me and love me like a Father to his children. In this struggle I hear so softly his words "David, come to me. Let me embrace you. For I love you" An aura of incredible peace seeps through my soul as the essence of love takes hold of me. The Glorious Creator, the giver of Love receives my love, the surrender of my soul to his will and obedience! In this spirit of thanksgiving and worship I am strengthened to witness to others the glory of God. St Paul writes in Colossians: Being strengthened with all the power according to his glorious might so that you may have great endurance and patience joyfully giving thanks to the Father.

It is in my contemplation that I constantly remember the holiness, and the glory of God. This strengthens and activates me to be his worthy witness. Without this contemplation I can forget God and become more lost and homeless. Perhaps what I am saying here is I can only do "glorious" things for God when my heart and soul is truly with God.

Before I close this meditation the elect city of God with all its glory is also the city of great suffering. It is the city where Jesus was crucified and the temple was destroyed. This is a reminder that walking within the glory of God can also be a place of suffering. This can be a price of love. There is an old English saying- you cannot have a rose garden without the thorns. To truly follow God means taking up the cross of love if we want to do Glorious things for God.

GOD BLESSED THE WORDS SPOKEN

I cried out to him with my mouth; his praise was on my tongue. If I had cherished sin in my heart, the Lord would not have listened; but surely the Lord has listened and heard my voice in prayer. Praise be to God, who has not rejected my prayer or withheld his love for me!
[Psalm 66:17-20]

Words were spoken; and God blessed the words because the heart did not love sin. Does this imply that if God does not answer he has not listened because our heart is not pure? Often in prayer there is silence; just as there is silence between two lovers. A response is not necessary for they know one another. Just being in the presence with one another is sufficient for there is trust and desire. So it is in prayer we know that God is ever present and he hears but it is for him to speak. As our relationship with God grows ever warmer and stronger there is a deep sense of trust that we are walking with him. He is ever at our side. If we should drift towards sin; he will drift away from us until our soul has been purified in repentance. He will not leave us; like the father in the prodigal son he will wait for our "returning" – to the home of love of which the heart is the center. When we hunger and desire for the affections of love we cry out in longing, seeking the adoration that can be given and received; our heart craves to be filled with the passion of the beloved's love. Of all the things we cherish is the embrace of our beloved arms of warmth and protection. Our heart is living the romantic dance of life where joys and blessings are its candle of light erasing the shadows of anxiety and doubt. Loneliness gives way to the sheer delight of being in the presence of our beloved. God is love! He exists for love. We must desire and cherish him first. We can only be truly in his presence when our hearts are both pure and we seek him with all our heart. In such a place there is no room for sin. Our God is a jealous loving God. We cannot therefore serve two masters. Which we follow the God of love or the God of Self-serving. Our mouths will only speak of one of these Gods and our ears can only listen to the voice of one. Listen to what you speak and what you hear and you will know which God you follow.

GOD RESTED; WHY DON'T WE?

On the seventh day God had finished his work so he rested from all his work. [Genesis 2:2] So I declared an oath in my anger, they shall never enter my rest. [Psalm 95:11] So let us do our best to enter that rest. For the word of God is alive and powerful. It is sharper than the sharpest two-edged sword, cutting between soul and spirit, between joint and marrow. It exposes our innermost thoughts and desires. Nothing in all its creation is hidden from God. Everything is naked and exposed before his eyes and he is the one to whom we are accountable. [Hebrews 4:11-13

If our Lord, our sovereign and creator found time to rest from all his work, how come we find it so difficult? I am sorely tempted to say that some of us idolize motion. We are caught up in the drug called "speed". Whether it is in our car, speedboat, plane, skateboard, Hummer" or skies; the sheer joy of motion brings sheer ecstasy to our souls. For many, work and motion has become a prison, a barrier of life, as they struggle to reduce their mountain of debt; so they can retain the material well being they so covet. For a few the idea of tranquility suggests sloth and laziness. Even when we do "relax" we need to be entertained with sports, movies, and television. It is not that any of these activities are in themselves wrong; what appears to be missing is the "resting" of our soul. It is true that sleep rests the soul; as long as it is "restful".

Think for a moment when was the last time, we truly gave rest to our heart. By this I mean to be able to live just in the present, to enjoy the moment, and to be thankful for what you have- To acknowledge the "goodness" around you; and to thank God for his goodness.

Sadly, there is a tendency to live the Epicurean that leads to self-worship and Narcissism where little time is spent acknowledging God. We become like spoilt self-centered kids lacking compassion and care for others. Only we matter, the rest are not our concern. It is when we have divided the worlds between us and them that God's anger reaches the point that we will not be allowed to enter our rest and will forever live in tension, anxiety and arrogance. Unless we are prepared to change and acknowledge with contrite heart the love of God and asks for his forgiveness. Remember: Nothing in all its creation is hidden from God. Everything is naked and exposed before his eyes and he is the one to whom we are accountable. He knows the condition of our hearts.

So, let us take a "time-out" from our activities and take a "time-in" with God. Let him speak to us and in his mercy and grace his touch will erase the anxiety of our heart and allow us to be at peace. Just think would it not be wonderful for just a moment to be able to step away from the frenzy of modern life activity and to experience only the beat of our heart; to be able to say "life is good, thank you God". The word of God is alive, powerful, certain and eternal. If we listen carefully, we will discern it is restful and peaceful!

GOD'S JOYFUL MERCY

Bring joy to your servants for to you O Lord I lift up my soul. You are kind and forgiving O Lord, abounding in all who call on you. Hear my prayer, O Lord listen to my cry for mercy – [Psalm 86:3-7]

There is nothing remarkable for wanting joy. It is a natural desire to live in happiness and to delight in our surroundings and to obey our call. There is peace in our soul. Our hearts are indeed at rest. Our spirit is filled with laughter and mischief. We are walking in the warmth of love.

Yet it is the dance of life that at times we must walk in the darkness known as the "night of the soul"; if our faith is to grow strong. When all seems lost, where hope gives way to hopelessness, where faith falls into the shadow of despair and where joy evaporates to anger. The sweet fruit of love is eaten by the sour bitterness of discord. Concern for others is gone as we berate ourselves for our condition.

The storm clouds of discontent batter our soul with grievance upon grievance, convincing us we must be forsaken and that God does not care. We have become miserable wretches of doom. Life has become a struggle as long as we remain in this place of darkness and doom. It is time like this that faith is tested and we need to continue to look up and cry for God's mercy. We need to urge God to come to our time of need.

It is a test of faith to rid ourselves of our pride and control. We need to prostrate ourselves before God, repenting of our sins and exclaiming "We cannot do it alone; Lord, come I need your love, your kindness and your consolation". In truth God wants to help us; but we must call him first; but only in a spirit of humility. It takes a humble person to acknowledge help is needed; but it takes a repentant person to actually ask for help. It is a person of faith who believes and loves his God in times of trouble; for that person knows God is the anchor and the Hope- The anchor of foundation whose word are solid and eternal; and the Hope of eternal salvation for those who believe and obey

If there is any doubt as to God's love, generosity, love and kindness, we only have to look again on baby Jesus. As we reflect, pray and bow and head in awe we are truly aware of the historical significance of this historical hallowed event. Our redeemer, our Immanuel has come to bring joy and eternal life to us. In his love and innocence his blood will be bled for our freedom! Let us not forget, but in total obedience and adoration follow his path of unconditional love.

GOD'S DOORKEEPER

I would rather be a doorkeeper in the house of my God than dwell in the tents of the wicked. (Psalm 84.10)

The other day I was standing by my study door frame looking at the amazing early morning sky that was so transparent through the windows; when my eyes glanced on this verse in the bible I was holding in my hand; I saw the word doorkeeper. It struck me as a very odd word and when I looked it up in the index, I was puzzled to see this was the only time this word was used. So, what does it mean to be a doorkeeper in the house of God? Does it have any relevance?

I rolled up my sleeves, so to speak and started to study this word. I discovered like the wine- tasters the doorkeeper had a very important position. In Old Hebrew times the doorkeeper was a job given to the most capable, loyal and trained priest. His job was to ensure that no one entered the temple, who was unclean or undeserving. The purity of the temple was to be preserved. No infiltration of evil was allowed that could defile the temple. This doorkeeper's integrity allowed him to be in God's "approximant presence" not intimacy, but just so close to it that only a small fraction of humanity could ever experience. What a position of honour! The doorkeeper was the protector of temple purity rather than bouncer. This meant the doorkeeper had to have the highest integrity morale standard. What does this mean today?

Today of course with the work of the risen Christ we are the temple of God. The veil has been torn aside; we have access to the inner chamber. Through the spirit Christ he is in us here and now for all who believe in him. Through his work of grace, forgiveness, and love we now have a personal relationship with God the Creator. We have life and purpose, meaning and hope.

But the infiltration of evil is ever present. It challenges our thoughts, beliefs and actions. The function of doorkeeper is still desperately needed; even though its role has changed. It is now more ambassadorial. We are therefore Christ's ambassadors, as though God were making his appeal through us. We implore you on Christ's behalf: Be reconciled to God. God made him who had no sin to be sin for us, so that in him we might become the righteousness of God. (2 Cor.5:20-21). Come near to God and he will come near to you. Wash your hands, you sinners and purify your hearts, you double minded. Grieve, mourn and wail. Change your laughter to mourning and joy to gloom. Humble yourselves before the Lord and he will lift you up (James 4:8-10). The doorkeeper resides if you will at the entrance to our heart.

Whenever we harden our hearts to the love of God the spirit of God cannot heal us for the doorkeeper has shut the door so that God's love cannot penetrate; for the heart of love can never be tarnished by our impure condition. Left unhealed we will remain in the tents of the wicked in unrepentant willfulness. When we do turn our eyes from the impure, from the unjust acts, from out of our selfish desires to humble ourselves before God then the doorkeeper will open the door of our hearts to allow God's love into our heart. God is the eternal compassionate forgive waiting to embrace us in his arms of love! All we need is to knock, the door will be opened and we will receive the eternal love of the Master.

GOD'S LOVE REDEEMS THE REPENTANT

Help God- the bottom has fallen out of my life!
Master hear my cry for help!
Listen Hard! Open your ears!
Listen to my cries for mercy (Psalm 130:1-2)
As it turns out, forgiveness is your habit
And that's why you are worshipped (Psalm 130:4)
O Israel, wait and watch for God-
With God's arrival comes love
With God's arrival comes generous redemption (Psalm 130:7)

We all have our blue days where hope seems so distant. Nothing is going right! Calamity after calamity defines the day! It is one of those days you might just as well have stayed in bed. Like the psalmist you feel the bottom has fallen out of your life. What an excellent setting this is for the spirit of Self- pity to engulf your soul accompanied by its ardent supporters of groaning and moaning! I know this happens for in my constant introspection moods I love to admonish myself with much vigour of judgment and cursing that inevitably leads to self-centeredness and joylessness! But this is not the way of the psalmist. The first two words speak volumes about his heart. He cries out Help God.

It is the cry of the infant wanting his mother's comfort! It is the cry of the lover wanting to be embraced by the beloved! In this instance it is the psalmist seeking the blessing of his Abba Father. The psalmist eyes look outwards towards the one who can give mercy and help him in his despair! It is an action of faith in the hope that God will listen and show his healing hand. It is the mark of the repentant to acknowledge a mistake has been made and needs God's help to redeem the situation.

How we acknowledge our sins is critical! If as I have done so often, is to turn inwards and through self-talk, and bursts of emotional protestations I find my mood turns to a happier one. but this is only temporary. Why? You can never forgive yourself without true and real repentance. We can never be free of our guilt until we have asked God for mercy (act of confession). The psalmist looks beyond himself and calls on the one he trusts to listen and to help him. His trust and love for his God is a very distinctive hallmark of the psalmist relationship. He worships his God with all his soul, strength and body!

His life experience has shown that whenever he falls and comes humbly with confession and repentance God will forgive! This is a lesson for me and for each one of us that we come in true heart and contriteness and confess with honesty and integrity God will be forgiveness. This demonstrates the very essence of God; He is love! His Love is eternal and deep!

    The question for me is how great is my Love for God! Do I see him as my Abba Father, the one who created me, the one who is my shepherd and the one who loves me! The psalms show the deep relation that David had with his Father in Heaven. David was not perfect and when found out he responded with deep humility and sorrow. God loved David even with all his imperfections! God loves to redeem the repentant, through his act of gracious, generous forgiveness. This Psalm definitely challenges my relationship with my Abba Father.

GOD'S TRUTH IS THE WAY!

Surely, you desire truth in the inner parts; you teach me wisdom in the inner most places [Psalm 51:6] Hear my teaching; listen to the words of my mouth [Psalm 78:1].

We live in a world where truth is suspect, for "truth" appears to change with the "situation". The relativists assert there is no absolute truth. The absolutists are seen as intolerant, exclusive and archaic. Why do we indeed then seek truth?

To live in a world without truths is to live in a nihilistic world where moral code is nonexistent. It would be a place of darkness, fear and trembling. We need truth to live in security and to know we are loved by our neighbor and we in turn love our neighbor. Jesus said, "I am the way and the truth and the life".

To believe, to commit and to follow Jesus goes beyond just morality it involves transformation of our whole soul. It is the affection, the motivation to seek truth into our heart, into our most inner parts.

There is no attitude of passivity but an urgent energy to imitate him and to love him, for what he has done, what he has said and what he has promised. Our eyes are fixed on him; our ears listen to hear his words; our mouth speaks his words of love and compassion; and actions demonstrate our love to our neighbor. As we come more like him, we absorb the wisdom of his truth; it becomes our beacon on the path of truth. We become like children listening with respect and love to the words of the Father. All we can say is "Father, teach me…."

This is the wondrous truth of love that we have with God, who is our Father and we are his Sons and Daughters when we accept and seek his truth. Sadly, when such a loving relationship between parents and children is absent, it is so difficult to find this relationship without our heavenly father. Yes, we may desire such a truth but detachment so protects our hearts that connections become impossible. Love is feared; trust is unbelievable and belief is broken. Wisdom cries out in such circumstances that we must allow the presence of God's love to touch our souls and we will in time open our hearts to him. Patience in God's grace is indeed a virtue and is the beginning of wisdom and is the seed of desire.

This is the wisdom that lies behind the words in Psalm 79; for David knew too well that to walk God's path in his footsteps is the only true path of light, hope and love! Let us follow this path for the sake of our soul!

GRACE- MESSAGE THAT BLOSSOMS

*The wilderness will rejoice and blossom; like the crocus it will burst into bloom; it will rejoice greatly and shout for joy. [Isaiah35:1-2].
Your lips have been anointed with grace, since the Lord has blessed you forever. [Psalm 45:2].
May your unfailing love be my comfort. [Psalm 119.76ff]*

For weeks now I watched the flower buds in my container anxious to bloom; but cloudy skies one after another and incessant rain bursts have kept the lips of the bud closed protecting the flower within. As the days passed the buds looked more dejected, hanging awkwardly from the heavy rain drops on their thin stems and looking very colourlessly in their green garment; that I wondered if they were lost. Then without warning a sun ray surrounded the container and with this warm embrace I could see the flower buds gently lift upwards to receive this heated sustenance; slowly but surely from the caress of the sun the lips of the buds gently opened to expose a most delicate yellow flower with the most complex precise design possible. In awe I watched this change from a dull drab plant to one of sheer beauty. Such is the power of the sun!

I intuitively realized this must be how grace works in our lives. God's love is such that he never imposes or takes us for granted. He waits for us to receive him; to embrace if you will the light of truth. By accepting the comfort of his touch; the Holy Spirit touches our lips and anoints us with grace. This allows our souls to be transformed from a spirit of dullness to one of sheer joy and rejoicing. Because of this heated kiss God's blessing can now begin to in-bide in our heart allowing our true colouring to come forth in radiant brilliance; comforting, supporting and praising all that we meet. Fundamentally we have not changed. We are still the same person.

What has happened is that the flower within us has now been released opened up by the power and warmth of God's grace. The lips of doubt, that protected our true self from exposure, have vanished before God's love. We have become what God meant has to be- A person of compassion loving his neighbour and glorifying his God. Just as the blossoming of one flower is followed by the community of other flowers, so does the blossoming of one person full of grace impact the blossoming of grace in the lives of people in his community.

This to me is the mystery and the wonder of G.R.A.C.E. It is G (a gentle gift from God. It is rich and radiant in its presence). It is A (awesome in its serenity and beauty). It is C (comforting in its compassionate love). It is E (exuberant in its display of praise).

Each flower has been chosen with its colour and design; so it is that when we are filled in God's grace we have adopted the colour and design if you will what God has chosen for our path in life. Grace is indeed the messenger that enriches our lives. When grace is in us we simply bloom with sheer radiant beauty fully praising and rejoicing with joy God's name!

HE MAKES ME LIE DOWN IN GREEN PASTURES

He makes me lie down in green pastures.
He leads me besides still waters
He restores my soul (Psalm 23:2)

I love this passage! Just reading the words slows me down; the world seems a calmer place; and the storms of life have been replaced by a warm breeze of comforting reassurances.

There was a time, in my childhood when I would on a sultry hot summer day lie down in the hay field with a straw in my mouth gaze at the majestic billowing cumulus clouds with a vivid blue sky as its backdrop floating with the greatest at ease through the endless space; nearby I could hear the gurgling of the water in the creek flowing to a distant delta; dragon flies would buzz above my head before darting to another place; the gentle breeze massaged my tensions; and eventually my eyes would become heavy with sleep! Immersed in God's creation I felt secure and fearless. It was indeed a wonderful restful time!

The Psalmist reminds me to be "restored" is to follow two conditions: To lie down in green pastures and to lead me besides still waters. Like sheep I can only stop being restless, tense, fearful and anxious and lie down when I am "free of all fear". This is the role and characteristic of the Good Shepherd. When the sheep has its eye on the Shepherd they trust, their fear will dissipate and they will lie down. I know I will pace and be wary until my eyes are on the one, I can trust. A spirit of peace will seep through my soul when this occurs. It is because of the sheep and my trust that "makes" us want to obey and follow the Shepherd. So, it is with our Lord and Sovereign that because he is a God of compassionate love, he never denies us the freedom to make our choices; God never forces us to do anything we don't want to do! Of course, we have to live with the consequences of our choices. The joy of lying down before the Lord comes when we are in a spirit of solitude where our soul and mind is focused on Him. It is at this time the hustle and bustle of life noises and concerns give way to the Spirit of discernment and peace as we wait to hear the Lord's word. In hand in hand God leads us to the "still waters" of his love. This love is not a passive love of inertia; it is the active love that is generous in spirit as we share it with those who are needy.

My soul is "restored" when God's perfect love has cast out my fears and my faith has been transformed to truly trust and love God. My prayers will be empowered where my faith and my love dominate my heart. I will know this when I can say the words written by Paul with all my heart and soul:

I have learned the secret of being content in any situation, whether fed or hungry, whether living in plenty or in want. I can do everything through him who gives me strength (Philippians 4:12-13)

Paul learnt how to lie down with the Lord and by the still waters of faith to spiritually be hand in hand with his Shepherd so that he was restored daily where love perfectly cast out fear and anxiety and peace ruled in his love because of God's compassionate eternal love! May this also be in my life!

HEARTACHE OF SELF-LOVE CRUSHES THE SPIRIT

They close up their callous hearts and their mouth speaks with arrogance. [Psalm 17:10] I will praise the Lord, who counsels me; even at night my heart instructs me. Therefore my heart is glad and my tongue rejoices, my body also will rest secure. [Psalm 16:7 and 9]. Teach us to number our days aright, that we may gain a heart of wisdom [Psalm 90:12]

I sometimes wonder whose glory I promote-Myself! God! Indifference! This is an important question to answer for it reflects the condition of my heart. If my heart is closed only to self, where all thoughts are self-thoughts, where all knowledge are self-knowledge, I will soon fall into the spirit of self-love which inevitably leads to self-hate. My attitude to others will become cold, insensitive and my heart will indeed become callous and the words I speak will be opinionated and arrogant. Self-inflicted reclusion will become my lot as I will be perceived to be anti-social, miserly and unloving. My life will become full of every kind of wickedness, sin, greed, hate, envy, murder, quarrelling, deception, malicious behavior, and gossip. I will become a backstabber, hater of God, insolent, proud and insolent.

Why? Because I knew my God but chose not to worship him and in disobedience my mind became confused and dark as I followed my own idols and gods. My promises are mere paper-tigers and have no substance; and my heart will lack love and mercy. When I constantly glorify myself it can only lead to one path – a heart of callousness and unfeeling.

The only way to prevent this is to open my heart to the word of God. A happy heart makes the face cheerful, but heartache crushes the spirit. I daily thank God for his grace and mercy. Yes, I may sin from time to time, but in repentant spirit I return to him for forgiveness and love. While indeed I have a long way to fully appreciate and embrace this unconditional love, I know he is working in my heart. His spirit is an anchor of conscience and wisdom in my heart, instructing me how to live like a child of God so that I might imitate my God and Savior. In this way the love of Jesus abides in my soul!

This is why my face can reflect the radiance of God's love, my words can speak the praises of my beloved, and my soul is at rest as if it is in the arms of my Father in heaven. Each day the fragrance of God's love soaks the spores of my soul that leaves me in a spirit of awe and longing. I can truly trust in the Lord!

I WILL TAKE REFUGE IN THE SHADOW OF YOUR WINGS

I will take refuge in the shadow of your wings [Psalm 57:1] Where is the house you will build for me? Where will my resting place be? [Isaiah 66:1] I have loved you with an everlasting love; I have drawn you with loving kindness. I will build you up again and you will be rebuilt [Jeremiah 31:3-4].

Whenever I feel anxious, I tend to go to places of safety like my home or the innermost place of my soul. Where I feel the most secure these are my places of "refuge". They are places I know well for they bring rest. What does the psalmist mean when he says "I will take refuge in the shadow of your wings"? To imagine you are holding on to the wings of an eagle, as I have done, is to experience the power and the strength of this awesome bird. To be in the shadows of the wings suggest you are in the cleft where the wing attaches to the body. In faith and loving fear you hold onto the wing knowing you cannot be touched and yet your life depends on the eagle. I confess that with all my imagination I do not consider this as a place of rest. Yet our souls are nomadic, restless, and ever seeking for that house of rest, where love and kindness is received. It is a house where abandonment or loneliness is alien, for love is supreme.

Where do we find this love? - In the house of the Lord. God is love! He desires our worship and love in return. God is merciful and his kindness is everlasting. God is there when we fall from the path of truth. Like the gentle father he will pick us up and restore our souls. We need to have an open heart that seeks repentance, reconciliation and forgiveness for our sins. Our souls must be open to the spirit of God to draw into our hearts the loving embrace of God, so that we truly become the temple of God. In this transformation the love and kindness we receive from God we are able to transmit such love and kindness to those we meet and serve. When this occurs we have found our home and refuge. We are secure in the love of God. The paradox is that at the moment we have arrived, we want to change and adapt. God's message is clear that we are to be witnesses of God's love. That is to say the love we have received from God; we in turn must now be ambassadors of love to others. What do we do?

We add regulations, codes, practices and traditions to this love. All this does is move love from the inner heart to acceptance of human externalities. Love goes cold; the way to love becomes elusive. Joy is transformed to joyless. Love is transformed to despair. Freedom of worship is transformed to law's burden. Free Grace of God's love has been captured and bound by endless regulations and traditions. The simple message of love to love your neighbor as you love God has been lost to the cacophony of complex messages of the law. This is not what God intended; but God is merciful and when our hearts are ready to receive him he will "build us up again and we will be rebuilt". Let us pray in thankful hearts that he is there when we are not.

IN OUR DARKEST MOMENT THE LIGHT WITHIN IS OUR SENTINEL OF HOPE

You are the children of the light and the children of the day. We do not belong to the night or to the darkness.
(1 Thessalonians 5.5)
I wait for the Lord, my soul waits and in his word I put my hope (Psalm 130:5)
For when I am weak, then I am strong (2 Corinthians 12:10)
Why is my pain unending and my wound grievous and incurable? (Jeremiah 15:18)
You shall love the Lord your God with your whole heart, your whole soul, and your whole strength (Deut 6:5)

For over 40 nights my sleep has been disturbed by pain and for over 40 days this pain has reminded me of my frailty. Waves of frustration, anger and grief flies through me as I react to my inability to do the most simple of things. My thoughts are dark and stormy. I cry internally this is it! My time has come! I tell my friends that this pain has given me a new meaning to the "grouchy ole man". Even the support of friends has not ebbed the black mood that has captured my body and soul. Words of encouragement and caring suggestions has not improved my sombre mood. My soul is in the Dark Night of the soul struggling for meaning and feeling abandoned. I lie amok in a spirit of distress and loneliness where pain is my merciless mocking pest! I have lost count the nights I have woken up with pain that awakens me to utter darkness. There is no one there; I am alone in bed cast as a miserable forgotten septuagenarian! I cry out:

Why is my pain unending and my wound grievous and incurable?

Then in the darkest moment of my soul a light within me opens my ear to hear these words "Have you finished with your self-destructive spirit of self-pity? Have you forsaken me? Have you lost my love for you? With these words my soul is becalmed as I feel and experience the great sweetness of peace and loving friendship of God's hand on my heart. With these words I am reminded I can still Love God in my affliction. With these words I know I can endure the pain and my weakness for when I am weak, then I am strong in the abiding love of my God. With these words I am no longer a child of darkness, steeped in despair, I am transformed to a child of light bathed in its comforting rays of truth and hope. Indeed, the light within me is my sentinel guiding me to a place of comfort and of life!

Through this affliction I am learning more about the phrase "patience of waiting". Daily I relearn the meaning to wait for the Lord, for my soul waits with eagerness for his word; it is my hope. This hope is not born from the spirit of fatalism but from the love Christ constantly bestows on me. It is a love that sharply comes to focus as I am reminded that where I, as a wayward child might abandon my Lord; he never does. He is constantly at my shoulder graciously chiding me for my fickleness and through his love warmth guiding me on the path I must follow. It is a love not be possessed but to be freely given to others. With this change of focus my eyes turned outwards to show my care, concern and compassion for others. Slowly but surely the inner and physical pain I felt diminished as loving my neighbour conquered the darkness of the pain as the light of warmth love seeped through my soul seeing the joy my neighbour felt because of my affections!

This is only possible because you, Lord loved me first! Let me never lose this love! It is my desire to imitate you, in spite of my human failings, and to constantly walk in love, as you have loved me! My heart beats with wondrous love for I now know your spirit acts as a guard to my heart ensuring that I do not go astray; in this I am utterly humbled to be so loved and so blessed.

IN YOU LORD I BREATHE THE FRAGRANCE OF LOVE!

In your laws I delight; I will never forget your word (Psalm119.16)
The fear of the Lord is the beginning of wisdom! (Psalm 111.10)
He is our Father and in him we live and move and have our being. (Acts 17:28)

Today's world is very much one that is divisive and individualistic. The sense of wholeness has been erased by the passion for programs and processes of life. The technical beat of life has replaced the natural organic rhythm of life. The spirit of the technique has no place for the moral; it simply exists and will change without warning or concern of its results. It should not be a surprise that what we say differs from what we do. Truth in this situation merges with False until they both wear the same coat of morality. Is it no wonder the contemplative struggles to hear the word of God and to make sense of our turbulent ever increasing chaotic world?

In contrast to the busy, rushing, and noisy world the contemplative searches to discern the mystery of the unknowing cloud amidst a world that says all knowledge must be empirically proven. The idol of today is the God of Me-ism, of which the Selfie is its child. This concentration on the "I" has no room for the "Thou". In fact, the I and the Thou are merging into one because of our self-centered narcissistic attitudes; instead of man being in the image of God we see ourselves as simply being in the image of Self. Instead of how I can love and help my neighbour, the emphasis now is – What do I want in this life and what drum rhythm should I beat. Join me if you want but I am indifferent to your choice!

In such a world as this the mystery of the fear of God becomes meaningless and to follow God's precepts are of no value unless they coincide with the secular mindset. Why is this so! We live in a disposable world. Once a product has served its purpose; it is thrown away. Sadly this trend has moved into values. Love was once considered the highest of values but now it has become a commodity. To be used when wanted and then disposed of when a new relationship raises its head. Conflicts are more frequent as the strands of peace are torn and tethered as the sword of intolerance; anger and hatred display their hostilities. The world is simply at war with itself for without love only the dark clouds of judgments remain!

This is why the contemplative is needed so much! Their focus, joy and delight is to know and love God. In the cool quiet breeze of the dawn, in the soothing peace of night the contemplative can take time to reflect, to meditate with God, the Creator and the Shepherd of Life! The challenge is to find that quiet time, to close off all distractions and to be able to say Lord, I am here. I am listening! Let our hearts and minds focus on the goodness, mercy and grace of our sovereign Lord. Beware do not fall into the Spirit of Quietism, which Thomas Merton warns is dangerous for it leads to a false mask because our eyes are looking inwards instead of outwards to God. In such a stance we can fall into the messy mire of introspective self-talk and self- condemnation!

Our stance should be to meditate on the wonders and the mysteries of God's love, thanking Him for what He is doing in our lives and listening carefully to His word! As we do this allow our heart to be open and vulnerable; and permit our bodies to gently relax as the stress moves from our tight muscles and restrict throats to permit God's Sprit to massage our tired body with tender love and compassion. In the stillness of the moment the coolness in your heart will once again beat with fire of desire to love God for his sake and in turn you will love yourself more. In a very real way the Spirit of God is now living and moving within us. He is truly abiding in us; with this love we can go out and bring the fruit of this love to all we meet.

We will know when this is happening because our sensibilities have become more acute to the externalities around us- the wonders of the created world that needs healing, the goodness of people that are hurting, and the need for compassion to those that are suffering- that moves us to actively in love meet their needs. In this way the contemplative learns to die to self and become resurrected in love of God to help a hurting and dark world. The smaller our "I" becomes, the greater the "thou" of God is within us. The fragrance of His love will be an ever increasing and wonderful joy to us which we will delight in sharing to all we meet.

The journey of the contemplative is one of discipline, reflection and service. While there are times to be alone with God which is necessary for spiritual maturity; there is an absolute need for fellowship and friendship where accountability, education and affections are received and given. It is an awesome reminder that God's love works most effectively in community and by community.

Our individualistic world is in desperate need of new understanding of community love. The contemplative with eyes focused on the goodness of God can transfer this Spirit by their witness of warmth, compassion and grace. A sleeping hurting world can experience the joy of true community where neighbourly love is more important. The contemplative by their witness can give a ray of Hope to a fearful dark world that there is warmth, love and grace. In God's path there is light, truth and peace! The contemplative can indeed become the messengers of this loving Hope!

The time has come to change the world from the smell of death and the blood of war to one where it breathes the fragrance of God's Love! Let us contemplate on this delightful thought as we reflect on God's goodness to us.

JOYFUL FOREST BATHING IMMERSED IN THE SPIRIT OF GOD

Let us walk in the light of the Lord (Isaiah 2:5)
You will go out in joy and be led in peace;
The mountains and hills will burst into song before you,
And all the trees of the field will clap their hand
(Psalm 56:12)

Since the 1980's Japan has practiced the art of Shinrin-Yoku – Forest Bathing; which means going for a short visit to the forest to take time to soak in the surroundings of nature sounds, colours and shapes; which has been medically proven to prevent diseases and cancers by reducing stress levels. For years I have enjoyed the solitude of the forests.

There is something about the odour of the wood after a recent shower that permeates the air which fills your nostrils with its scented fragrance that reduces mental and physical tensions to loosen within you. The sounds of flowing waters and rustling leaves are joy to the ear which aids the overtaxed body to relax. The diversity of colour and shapes dance with exuberance before your eyes that turns your eyes from dull tiredness to one of child sparkling delight of wonder! The canopies of trees that cover the trails beckon you into their natural sanctuary of peace and solitude accompanied by gentle breeze that glides you into the forest glades. Sun rays wink between the trees teasing you with its warming glow. You cannot but help soak up the forest surroundings as it bathes you and cleanses you of daily tensions as the spirit of anxieties give way to a spirit of happiness!

It is in the forest trials or the path along the dykes that I feel closer to God. These are the moments when I sense him walking by my side. It is here I can say like Samuel "I am listening Lord, I am here". This is the time my soul is cleansed, as his gentle word eliminates the confusion that lies in my mind to replace it with clarity of focus that leaves my heart with a sense of wondrous joy, peace and purpose.

It is here I can sit on a rock or bench where time becomes timeless as I contemplate the wonder of God's creation and wait patiently for his word. It is here with eyes shut that I can sense his presence affirming that I am not alone! In this solitude I am in paradise. It is just me and Him enjoying each other's company! In such moments as this I am indeed bathed in God's spirit and cleansed by his words of encouragement. This is my Garden of Eden; it is my spiritual paradise. My time with Him, May it always be so!

It is with some amusement tarnished with a little irony that modern science in its obedience to the Spirit of Rationalism comes to same conclusion as our God, our Creator intended; that the forest be a place of harmony, joy and healing

And the Lord God made all kinds of trees to grow out of the ground- trees that were pleasing to the eye and good for food. God saw that all he had made, and it was very good.   Amen!

LORD RESTORE MY SOUL

HE IS MY HOPE AND COMFORT

LET THERE BE LIGHT

And God said, "Let there be light, and was light."[Genesis 1:3]. You, O Lord, keep my lamp burning; my God turns my darkness into light. [Psalm 18:28] For with you is the foundation of life; in your light we see light. [Psalm 36:9]. He reveals the deep things of darkness and brings deep shadows into the light. [Job 12:22]. The darkness is passing and the true light is already shining [1 John 2:8]. You are all sons of the light and the sons of the day. We do not belong to the night or to the darkness. [1 Thessalonians 5:5]

The very first thing we often see at dawn is the "new light of the day" as the Sun shows its face with radiant colors of yellow, crimson, and magenta streaks across the sky. As we know on the West Coast clouds often hide this light from us. The very first act written in the sacred scriptures is the creation of light by our God. Light is the source of energy; without it there is no life. It is not surprising that the Bible is full of metaphors and analogies on "light" and "darkness". These two words represent the spectrum extremes of "life" and "death".

We are encouraged to live in the "light" and to avoid the "darkness". Why is it necessary to have all these reminders? What does it mean to live in the "light"? Who has not met a person with a dark and cloudy disposition on a day that is full of sunny warmth and light? This person walks in "darkness" in a day "full of light". Nothing is going right; the world is a rotten place and I wish I was "dead". There is nothing like beating up our soul. Yet in our darkest moments we still seek that hope, that faith and that path that will bring us up out of the pit of despair. At this point of desperation and vulnerability we look beyond ourselves and with open heart and mind we see again the warmth, the love and the light of God.

It is as if the clouds of despondency and self-pity that create the darkness have now dissipated and all that there is the light of grace. For this to happen there must be a desire to repent, to ask for forgiveness and to renounce our sinful affections. We need to be purified before we can face our Savior the Lord. It takes steps. Each step revealed brings us closer to our salvation. At first the shadows appear as light comes through. We see the silhouette of our soul and our true condition is revealed. We pray, we contemplate and remain silent as we listen for God's word. In time we feel the warmth of his love and the soothing whisper of the Holy Spirit tenderly consoling us. We feel bathed in his love. We feel blessed in the heat of his light. Our soul becomes radiant in his love. –the darkness has passed and the true light is shining on us!

What has been hidden to us is now revealed. It is like standing on a hill looking at the valley below hidden in the shadows and then the light of the sun erases the shade and the details of the valley are revealed in its minutest details. So, it is with our soul as we allow God to heal our hearts, open our eyes he will reveal the wonders and the gifts that have been hidden in our soul. In awe and in joy we can rejoice in the power and mercy of God's light the path of salvation and eternal life.

LOST HEART IN A WORLD OF ME-ISMS

Give ear to my words O Lord, consider my sighing
Listen to my cry of help! (Psalm 5:1)
Do not merely listen to the word, and so deceive yourselves. Do what it says. (James 1:22)
Put your hope in God (Psalm 42:11ff)
How good and pleasant it is when brothers live together in unity....
For there the Lord bestows his blessing, even life forevermore (Psalm 133: 1 and 5)

Who has not woken up with a heavy heart and lead feet where a desire for life is lacking! You feel utterly alone; a spirit of futility has wrapped itself around your soul! A dark spirit, like the carrion crow call, invades your consciousness weakening your resolve to hope, believe and trust. All you can see is darkness, emptiness and even death. The light of hope seems so, so far away.

Recently I lost a friend who is now with the Lord! I am thankful I can celebrate the memories and the times we had together! There is an uncalled vacuum lying in my soul. I wonder who will be there for me when my time comes. Perhaps more pertinently, who will take the time to listen to my cry, to my loneliness? Where will I find consolation? Who will comfort me? Lonely dark path I travel is hard, brittle and barren of any form of encouragement. I have become a mere shadow that passes through the path of life that is perceived with indifference and apathetic fervour!

My spirit is caught in a vortex of joy, hope, despair, and anguish that love cannot penetrate my heart. All I want to do is lash out in snarling anger at this uncaring, un-listening world, where the cult of Me-isms reigns supreme. Where words are as deep as rice paper and love is as fickle as the current interest, loyalties and affections. How man likes to live in the spirit of Cain rather than the spirit of Love.

In my anguish and hurt I cry out to you for you are my only hope. Each passing day the meaning of life becomes more meaningless. The dark menacing clouds of doubt torment my soul by tormenting my soul with dripping mockery and sarcasms screaming the words: "You fool! Are you stupid? You became vulnerable? You attempted to trust them? Are you surprised you were ignored by acts of indifference? You got what you deserved! Never forget you are not beloved, their actions prove it."

No, I cannot believe this! Lord help me out of this mire of self-pity and self- condemnation. If my life is worth anything, let me never forget that you are my salvation, you are my teacher of truth, you are my shepherd of love; you are my light that leads me to truth! Oh Lord it can be so hard to simply desire love but it is so much harder to ask for love and to be ignored!

    Be thou my strength. Console my heart. Hold me dear to your heart O Lord so that I can hear its beat of compassion against my cold heart where love has gone astray.

MAJESTY OF GOD'S POWER IS SEEN AT THE PEAK

And to this day it is said "On the mountain of the Lord it will be provided" – Genesis 22:14
Who may ascend the hill of the Lord?
Who may stand in his holy place?
He who has cleans hands and a pure heart, who does not life up his soul to an idol or swear by what, is false. He will receive the blessing from the Lord – Psalm 23:3-5
The mountains will bring prosperity to the people. Psalms 72.3
The mountains melt like wax before the Lord – Psalm 97:5
How beautiful on the mountains are the feet who bring good news- Isaiah 52:7
Come let us go to the mountain of the Lord – Micah 4:2

On sunny days when the sky is incredibly clear and blue the view of Mount Baker is impressive with the beauty of its white capped peaks and by its sheer size and prominence. Its very presence magnetizes your attention! It is truly impressive. You cannot help but be in wonder at God's creation. There is something very spiritual about mountain peaks! You have a sense you are on the top of the world, close as you will ever be to heaven. You also are acutely aware of your own insignificance as your eyes survey the panoramic expanse below you. All you can do is to gasp and be in reverent silence. I have been there many times and for me it is truly a mystical experience. No wonder the mountain peaks are a holy and sacred place!

The peak is indeed a place of beauty, a place of blessings, a place of good news; but it is also a place of challenge and transformation. It is here at the summit that God is found! It is a place journey. If you have ever hiked up a mountain trail you know it can be very testing, challenging and tiring. It requires discipline, tenacity, and motivation. So, it is with our devotions and prayers. The trials and struggles are worth it for when you reach that summit, which seemed so impossible to reach, you are awestruck by the view. To me this is stepping off St. Bernard's top ladder rung of love; for indeed the presence of the Lord is felt. You feel his burning love as you realize the depth of the majesty and diversity of His creation! There is an extreme sense of gladness that you made it!

But the summit is a dangerous place, for the unprepared it can be fatal. Instant storms can surround the peaks without warning; a dark cumulus cloud can surround the mountain summit with a blanket of mist, mixed with winds of furies, thunder and lightning accompanied with monsoon rain or blizzards. Light and clarity vanishes before the darkness. Such is our spiritual journey for when we believe we have reached the summit of our spiritual journey dark spirits of doom, depression, doubt and discouragement can hurl itself on our soul, testing our faith, hope and belief.

At times like this we need to stay calm, and seek God's wisdom. Look at the words of the psalmist. We must become like the Thessalonians constantly thanking God for what he has done, what he is doing in our lives, and to be like the Ephesians and put on the full armour of God so that we can attain the fruits of the spirit as outlined in Galatians. Life is hard, the journey of life is challenging but the promises and love of God is eternal!

MY HEART PULSES WITH DESIRE

My body longs for you, in a dry and weary land where there is no water. I have seen you in the sanctuary and beheld your power and your glory; because your love is better than life [Psalm 63:1-2]. All my longings lie open before you, O Lord; my sighing is not hidden from you [Psalm 38:9]. What does the Lord your God ask of you but to fear the Lord your God, to walk in all his ways, to love him, to serve the Lord with all your heart and with all your soul, and to observe the Lord's commandments and decrees that I am giving you for your own good. [Deuteronomy 10:12]

Who has not walked in the heat of the sun, along mountain trails desiring the cool refreshment of water to reenergize our body? Or have driven all morning when you feel that emptiness in your stomach that tells you nourishment is required; so, you look with longing for your favorite restaurant. These are natural physical longings that are temporary, and vanish when we partake of what we desire. But there is a deeper longer, a longing that is so deep within our soul that it motivates us, energizes us and wraps us in its desire. It is the intense passions and longing of lovers, who breathe, dream and live for each other. The thought of being separated from one another is too much; the thought of doing something with each other gaze face to face with adoring intensity. Their love is such that they would give their lives to please their loved one. Love is the most passionate of all emotions. Their hearts are open and vulnerable - all their longings are open!

It is the same spirit and intensity of love that God seeks from us, except nothing is hidden. God knows – our sighing is not hidden from you. To truly love God, we must love him with adoration. St Bernard asks – Where is that longing, that intense love for God? For without this longing God becomes a mental abstraction, where personal relationship is impossible. As I read St. Bernard, I realize he is in love with his God. His mystical writings are intense in their mysticism of adoration; for him the incarnation of our Savior is reality. For me I lack this deep adoration. It seems I lack this affection for love, and without it my God seems so afar. It is not that I don't desire love; it is I do not love enough. It is not that I do not fear I just do not fear enough. It is as if I am at a crossroads hesitating between fear and love; undecided which way to travel.

What is this predicament that prevents my heart from sighing deeply for his presence and rest peacefully in the thought of God's love? It is I believe my self-love caused by a deep desire to protect my dignity and identity; from early experiences that love means abandonment and separation. While I long for God's love I find I cannot love him with all my heart; for my heart is torn. It is said that once the love of God has released you from self –love, the flame of divine love never ceases to burn in your heart and you remain united to God by an irresistible longing. St. Bernard states: the more surely you know yourself loved; the easier you will find it to love in return. In Matthew 5:8: Blessed are the pure in heart; for they shall see God. Again, St Bernard writes only the touch of the Holy Spirit teaches, and it is learned by experience alone. Let those who have not had this experience burn with desire, not so much to know as experience it.

While my heart pulses with alternating desire for love and my will desires to protect; my voice is silent because I am at the crossroads. I know I am a sinner and I have prayed before God for forgiveness. This has been a personal moment with God. I know I am not a trusting person. Love is so fragile for me. To pray before a priest who acts in persona Christi will require an act of trust, faith and love which I confess I do not have. I have protected self for so long that it would take a miracle to break down these walls of distrust and fear. In all my life I have never confessed to my mother, or to my father. My voice, out of defiance and fear to protect self, has always remained silent. This is my struggle. When will I be accepted for who I am? Why must I always prove what I am? Why is love so difficult? All I want is to love my God! My heart burns in the anger of constant proof when all I want is the love of God. Yes, I still live in a dry and weary land where there is no water and wonder whether the struggle is worth it- to turn my experience of love from alienation and abandonment to one of delight and joy.

O LORD YOU ARE MY GOD

O Lord you are my God, earnestly I seek you; my soul thirsts for you, my body longs for you, in a dry and weary land where there is no water. I have seen your sanctuary and beheld your power and your glory, because your love is better than life. [Psalm 1-2ff]

It is said that the depth of your love reflects the depth of your passion; so, it is with the love of God. Do we just lip serve the words out of some well-worn ritual that inevitably leads to meaninglessness? Or do we truly seek him with all our heart and love?

Reflect for a moment on the word "earnestly", for when a person is earnest there is a determined, tenacious, and purposeful spirit within him. A spirit of intense sincerity and feeling is invoked in his seeking of the Lord. It is as if every fiber and muscle in his soul is tensed to find his Lord. Why? Because his soul is dry and weary and lacks the water of salvation which sustains life. Who has not gone on a hike on a hot dry summer day, with a water bottle empty when the body soon feels dry and the throat parched? You seek the cool refreshing life-saving water of the stream. It is so, with the soul. There is time when, like Job, all seems lost and the spirit of grace has vanished. We are weary from the torments and wounds of life. Does our soul thirst for the waters of salvation? Does our body seek the hands of grace? Do we have a vision of God's power and glory? Or do we remain lost in our soul of self-pity and remorse? With powerful words the psalmist even in his sad predicament is able to rejoice in God's love because it is better than life.

The psalmist has a love of God that many of us desire, for our image of God's glory is too small and/or perhaps our fear of love is too great. Whatever the reason the awesome power of God's grace in our lives is weakened because of our resolve not to be vulnerable before him. God created man because of his love for Him; God desires Man to have loving relationships but many of us walk through this world looking for love. Our heart is empty for it seeks the love it does not have; and fears the love it seeks.

Through abuse, through abandonment, through a life of fear, and insecurity trust has evaporated and intimacy is feared above all else. So, we walk on the peripheral of life and become a shadow of what we should be in our life. Instead of God's love and compassion being greater than life in our soul; his love is kept at the edge of our life as we live on the edge of life. We spend time in nomadic dryness doing what we ought not to do when we know what we ought to do. To see the sanctuary of life is not enough we must touch this sanctuary by allowing the spirit of

God to tenderly enter our heart with tender love and compassion. To do this our heart must be open to receive this spiritual gift by humbling ourselves before him and with a spiritual mouth open the waters of salvation will refresh our dry soul. In wonder and in awe we will be surprised with utter joy the sense of peace that envelops us. Christ have mercy on us!

PASSAGE OF ADULTHOOD

How can a young man keep his way pure? (Psalm 119:9)
Young men will see visions (Joel 2:28)
Encourage the young men to be self-controlled (Titus 2:6)
Young men be submissive to those who are older (1 Peter 5:5)
He satisfies my desires with good things so That my youth is renewed like eagles (Psalm 103:5)

Every Spring I watch the young herons learning to fly. They tend to stand on the edge of the dyke water spreading their wings, flapping them with much vigour; jumping up and down; with short spurts they fly and land not too graciously. The herons know if they are to catch up to their parents they must fly. It is a dangerous time which can lead to injuries which are fatal as the predators; the eagles, the hawk, and the coyote watch and wait to pounce on them when they are most vulnerable. This is the heron passage of rite into adulthood; learn to fly or die! The young eagles passage of adulthood is similar, without warning their parents simply push them out of the nest; fly they must if they are to live!

As I reflected on this passage of adulthood, I remembered this was a time that gave me much anxiety and mental anguish. By the time I hit twenty I was alone; my parents were deceased; and I knew in my mind that I had to learn quickly what it meant to be a Man; but in my heart I had no real concept what it meant. Emotionally I was very much in a flap! The world to me was very unsafe, cruel and dark. There was no one I could go to because I was taught to be self- sufficient, a consequence of one of my father's dictates: Don't ask for help. There were many others: Don't talk so fast, don't admit you are confused, don't be a sissy act like a man, don't make eye contact with strangers, don't cry, don't touch; don't show your fears. Unfortunately, my father died without telling me what I could do to be an adult. To say I was confused is an understatement for I was expected to be an adult but I was simply living as a Man- child.

Constantly my body tormented me by reminding me that I was all male; but my mind thought as a child seeking the love and embrace of my mother who was no more. The time my mother and my father died within a year of each other was so traumatic I was changed forever! As I look back it was the darkest day of my youth; part of my heart simply died, the age of naivety and innocence was erased. I suffered in silence! I wept inwardly! I walked with slow heavy steps into a house that was void of any meaning. I should not have been alone but I was;

symbolic of my life. I did not feel the warmth of the sun for my soul and body was cold! I sat in the living room leaving the curtains closed; 1812 overture was played constantly. I drank myself to a stupor. Life had no more meaning!

My thoughts were of doom, darkness and nothingness. A spirit of hopelessness, directionless and emptiness held me in despair's vice. I had a bottle of my mother's sleeping pills by my side. It was full! I stared at these pills; and the more I stared: the more they seemed to hypnotize me to take them, eat them, and swallow them for they would be my escape route from the prison of loneliness that I felt so deeply. Such was the despair and the grief that had overwhelmed me. Slowly ever so slowly my hand reached for the pills. The moment I touched them the doorbell rang persistently. It echoed so loudly in my hurting head that I stumbled quickly to the door to silence this intrusion. I sharply opened the door and before I could say a word two arms took hold of me and hugged me for dear life! That act saved my life; a friend who cared took the time to come. When he saw me, my condition and how close to death I was his compassion was intense, gentle and understanding. We wept; I certainly wept more than I have done in my life for I had learnt that the world was not such a lonely place and people do care

This was my passage of rite into adulthood the Man-Child left me and I started to fly. My youth had been renewed, my spirit was full of hope and encouragement and I started to have visions- while not formalized I wanted to be an encourager!

REFLECTION OF DIVINE GLORY

Blessed is the man who fears the Lord
Who find great delight in his commands (Psalm 112:1)
Even in the darkness light dawns for the upright, for the gracious,
And compassionate man (Psalm 112:4)
He will have no fear of bad news;
His heart is steadfast, trusting in the Lord (Psalm 112:7)

The dawn is black as ink and all is quiet! I am sitting drinking my cup of tea and my mind has become stilled and yet on the other side of Earth there is turmoil, disaster, death and fear! A fear that you might be struck down by a tree, blown by the wind, turned upside down by a huge wave surge and knowing there is nowhere to hide. Three days Burma lived under such horrendous conditions of darkness, howling winds, flying objects that are too horrible for me to fathom. What is surrealistic is that I am calmly drinking my tea under peaceful conditions while my neighbour in dire straits has no power even to heat the water. Given these thoughts how do I reconcile the fear for the Lord with the fear of the unknown? How would I react where the possibility of death seems so imminent? How strong would my faith be in such a dark reality? Reading and reflecting on Psalm 112 gives me much insight to these questions!

Blessed is the man who fears the Lord! This is both a profound and perplexing statement. Profound in that it goes to the essence of the very nature of God. Perplexing in that in our minds fear means to run away from a situation that we believe will harm us. This does not make sense! God's very nature is to love. He is the all- powerful God that demands our awe and yet he seeks personal relationship with us. Like a lover to the beloved the attitude is one of awe and reverence sugared with sweet delight when we hear his word. The fragrant taste of God's word becalms our tensions and anxieties in a way no human endeavour can achieve. This is especially true when our heart truly appreciates the extent our Lord loves; to the point we can return that love with all our strength and might. In our secular world it takes incredible faith and belief to truly worship God in this truth: GOD TRULY LOVES YOU AND ME! The eternal mystery is when our heart truly intertwines with the Spirit of God's mercy and grace, our soul seeks most urgently for the sweetness of God's word for we delight in the feeding of God's commandment. In such a state our lips constantly praise the Lord with Hallelujahs of intense joy!

Our heart is open to receive his call! Our ears are attentive to his word! Our whole body dances in his spirit of God's love. We have become transformed to an internal light of God's grace, compassion and mercy which explodes externally by our glorious action of love and steadfastness to all we encounter! No amount of darkness, tragedy, uncertainty will break us from our God's love for the light of dawn is well and truly embedded in our hearts.

Sadly, we live in a world that does bad things, which can weaken our resolve to be obedient to God's love and call. Here the word says He will have no fear of bad news; His heart is steadfast, trusting in the Lord His heart is secure. This is indeed a mystery when all is dark and all is potent with the smell of disaster and death how is it possible to be steadfast. Above the clouds there is always the sun; and likewise, the beauty and strength of God's most tender love is the light that embraces our soul, not just our heart. It is with us when all is bright and when all is dark. It is a love that goes beyond human feelings; it is the spiritual love that looks to the divine; it is the powerful love that enabled Stephen to say "I see the heaven open and the Son of Man standing at the right hand of God"(Acts 7:56). It is a love that reflects the glory of God in your heart. It is a love that says you are never alone however stark the situation.

It is akin to the love of the Son who loved and

feared his Father. Jesus delighted in receiving the love of His Father; and the Father loved to delight in his son's love for he was well- pleased with his Son.

If we truly believe that God is love then we ought to love one another. Yet history, even today, abounds with Christian in their witnessing making judgment that rescinds the love. It is like receiving a gift and throwing it on the ground. This is so sad and unnecessary. We forget we are to give out love whatever, the situation by showing compassion, mercy and grace. If we do we will, from time to time, receive a reflection of the divine glory of what it means to be in the Kingdom of Heaven.

Let me close this meditation on Psalm 112 by quoting a small section of St. Bernard of Clairvaux Sermon 20 on the Song of Songs, Paragraph 2:

But there is something else that moves me, arouses and enflames me even more. Good Jesus, the chalice you drank, the price of our redemption, makes me love you more than all the rest. This alone would be enough to claim our love. This, I say, is what wins our love so sweetly, justly demands it, firmly binds it, deeply affects it. Our Savior had to toil so hard in this, in fact in making the whole world the Creator did not labor so much. Then he spoke and they were made; he commanded and they were created. But in saving us he had to endure men who contradicted his words, criticized his actions, ridiculed his sufferings, and mocked his death. See how much he loved us. Add to this the fact that he was not returning love but freely offering it. For who had given him anything first, that it should be returned to him? As St John said: "Not that we had loved him, but that he first loved us". He, loved us even before we existed, and in addition he loved us when we resisted him. According to the witness of St Paul: "Even when we were still his enemies we were reconciled to God through the blood of his Son." If he had not his loved his enemies, he could not have had any friends, just as he would have had no one to love if he had not loved those who were not.

This is powerful! We cannot be steadfast in isolation. God is a God of relationship his divine love pours out in action. If we do not love our enemies how will they come to know God's Divine love. If we keep God's love bound in our soul, we will have thrown away his gift in the trash heap of Sloth. If we want to see the reflection of Divine glory then this is the way

Christian, learn from Christ how you ought to love Christ. Learn a love that is tender, wise, and strong; love with tenderness, not passion, wisdom, not foolishness, and strength, lest you become weary and turn away from the love of the Lord. Do not let the glory of the world or the pleasure of the flesh lead you astray; the wisdom of Christ should become sweeter to you than these. The light of Christ should shine so much for you that the spirit of lies and deceit will not seduce you. (Sermon 20 para 4 St. Bernard)

Know, therefore, that in our darkest dreaded moments we are not alone for the reflection of divine glory lies in our heart if we eat his word, and drink his Spirit of grace!

LORD RESTORE MY SOUL

I AM WITH YOU ALWAYS

SENIORS WITNESS OF INNER LOVING LIGHT

Just as each day brims with your beauty, my mouth brims with praise. But don't turn me out to pasture when I am old or put me on the shelf when I can't pull my weight. (Psalm 71:8-9)

It was a beautiful hot arid summer day as we drove to see Aunt Lily. I was 14 years old. I have never met Aunt Lily but mother told me she was bedridden and had been so for most of her life. She had severe rheumatism and could not walk, and needed constant help in all things. As we drove through the driveway and up the circular Georgian driveway bordered with massive Rhododendrons fragrant with scent and diversified in colours of red, orange and purple, I wondered what it would be like to spend your life in bed. The thought horrified me. It would be like a prison. The idea of immobility was like a death sentence for one so full of unstoppable energy. The car stopped in front of grey scarred steps. My parents, sister and I got out of the car to meet the formal but genteel Matron and we followed her all the way up the stairs and down the corridors. I swear I can still hear the creaking sound of her stiff starch uniform. The smell of ammonia and other common hospital senses assaulted my senses which made me grimace that caused my mother to send an oral rebuke to me to behave. Dark shadows flitted alongside us and sometimes behind as we walked briskly towards Aunt Lily rooms and then we arrived at her door. Matron opened the door and we all walked in with me last of all. I am not sure what I was expecting but it was not good. But I was surprised. The room shone with brilliant sunlight; dust motes dancing with frenzy in the light shaft. Before me was a large bed with white quilt over it. There sitting, held by a number of pillows was a silver head lady with the most beautiful almost angelic smile and radiant face. Her voice was strong and full of laughter. Around her neck was the most extricate wooden cross I have ever seen. Her hands were all distorted from her illness; but it was with these hands I learnt later she made the most remarkable embroidered napkins and dolls. Then she saw me, we gazed at one another with much intent. I felt her warmth and her love. "So, this is David. I have longed to meet you. You have made me so happy. Come closer so I might see you more clearly." I walked to her bed, and sat on its edge and looked once more at Aunt Lily. She was so fragile, so beautiful, so full of gracious spirit and so very warm. I wanted to hug her but was afraid to; but in a spontaneous impulse of love I kissed her cheek. And then ran to the window with my back to all so they could not see my tears. I wondered how could someone so beautiful be bound so and felt that God had abandoned her; but when I looked at her again there was so much love in all she expressed that this could not be true. I realized the fears and angst I felt said more about me than her. To this day after some 50 years my one and only visit to Aunt Lily has left me with an unforgettable memory of beauty, love and suffering.

Aunt Lily spent almost 70 years bedridden. She was beloved by all who met and looked after her. When I asked how she could be so happy. She replied, "I may be bedridden but I still have my eyesight, I can hear well, I am well looked after and my room is more than sufficient and look at my view of the valley and sea; it is magnificent. Above all my Lord is constantly at my side. We have wonderful conversations. I can't wait to see Him." Given the impact Aunt Lily gave me on just one visit; what an awesome impact she must have had on all she met.

The psalmist words reminded me so eloquently that while our physical body may weaken it is the beauty of our inner soul that counts. Like the colours of the dying leaves which are vibrant in their reds, yellows and magenta before falling to feed the earth; so, it is that the spirit of our older people with their beauty of tenderness, compassion and love leaves a spirit of joy and peace in their wake. This is the beauty of life that our Lord has so intricately created.

From the birth of the new infant whose innocence and vulnerability give so much joy to the new family; so does the vulnerability, the tenderness, the love of the inner spirit of our seniors' pass a love that is beyond all understanding. This is the journey of life where each stage has its God - given gifts. The wondrous gift of seniors is to declare God's power to the next generation through the beauty of their loving gentle witness.

In our materialistic world where progress and action are sought above all things and there is little patience for those who are on the margin of society. With faith on the material alone the future is often unpredictable and tumultuous, and the now can leave us in a constant state of fear and angst. Hope is a non- existent entity. We seek a refuge that cannot be found. Love becomes a luxurious commodity as violence takes over. It is only when we turn to God for his mercy does salvation and hope become possible. Our seniors through their faithful life of service are the light to show the way for those who want to follow the light; because by their action they are indeed God's witness.

My Aunt Lily is my light and inspiration, for her beauty and her mouth praised constantly the love of God in her life. It is my prayer just as she has inspired others to follow the Lord by her life witness; I pray I will do the same in my life!

SILENCE AND SOLITUDE THE TWIN BEAMS TO DIVINE LOVE

It was a hot sultry sunny summer morning on the West Coast. Dawn had arrived! Huge clumps of cumulus clouds floated majestically against the deep blue sky. Crying screeches of the sea gulls with the shrill screeches of the eagles deadened the soothing sounds of waves crashing onto the sandy rocky beach. The panoramic views of the rugged coast line gave testimony to the force of nature. I was sitting alone on the tor point of the headland, hands in my pockets and legs braced around the rock which was supporting my body. I could feel the warm air buffeting my body as the sea gusts swept inland. I shut my eyes feeling the warmth of the sun massage my tense body. In time the sounds of the waves and the seagulls became muted; even the touches of the winds seemed softer. My mind ever alert, in progressing one thought upon another slowly ebbed to an eerie silence. I sensed the tensions in my muscles gently ease. The sounds around me intensified as the sounds within me became more acute. My eyes while open closed themselves to the external world and instead open themselves to my inner-self. I could sense the rushing of the blood bringing life to my organs. I could sense the beating of my heart as it pulsated the flow of blood to my organs that was just right to keep me alive. My heart beat faster as I thought how fragile my body really was as it relied on this small organ- the heart of life! The beat of the heart was almost hypnotic in its constant rhythm. Then inexplicably I sensed a presence within. It seemed to beat in concert with my heart beat! It felt wonderful! As I remained in this spiritual trance afraid to move a voice seemed to say ever so quietly "Be still. Be not afraid. My heart is on your heart! My love is rushing through your blood of life. You are not alone! Follow me! Love me as I have loved you! My eyes suddenly spring open. The coastal vista still lay before me as before. I pinched myself. It hurt! Good! But how was I to explain this mystery? I cannot! I am alone yet not alone! My soul felt peaceful! I cannot discern what I experienced except to believe God had spoken to me. I did not question it enough. My soul knew it had found its spiritual home. The father had spoken to the prodigal son!

    This vision is the one that I hold close to my heart. It is the desire of the pilgrim desiring to be home with his heavenly Father. I say vision for I have not yet reached the spiritual discernment that allows the silence of my mind and the solitude of my spirit to be truly the beams that guide me to divine love. I am an impatient person, ever on the move, with high energy that demands action; which all leads to a high expectancy for an immediate answer. I have not learnt the skill that requires you to sit quietly, to relax and wait for the spirit to speak to you. My mind is as restless as my body. I am like the deer that is ever alert for danger, quivering with nervous anticipation, quick to respond and ready to leap on any threat! This does not mean I do not think; I think deeply! It is best done while walking through nature's trails. Frequently I am motivated in the early dawn to express my thoughts in writing; it is as if during my sleeping hours my thoughts have worked over time.

The one thing I have learnt on my pilgrimage journey is that if there is no love in my heart the journey is pointless. The rebuke of Jesus to the Jewish Leaders comes to mind: Your approval means nothing to me, because I know that you don't have God's love within you; for I have come in my Father's name and you have rejected me. Yet if others come in their own name you gladly welcome them. No wonder you can't believe! For you gladly honour each other, but you don't care about the honour that comes from the one who alone is God. [John 5:41-44] Contemplation without belief whether it is done in silence or solitude will not bring you to the truth when love is absent in the heart.

This is why I love to read the psalms for every emotional condition of man is expressed but the central foundational trend of the psalm is the heart of love for his father! David knew how to speak to his Lord. Many a time David sought the solitude of his

Father in heaven and cried for God's mercy:

Hear my prayer, O Lord! Listen to my cries for help! Don't ignore my tears; for I am your guest- a traveler passing through, as my ancestors were before me. Leave me alone so I can smile again before I am gone and exist no more. [Psalm 39:12-13]. David's heart sought the heart of God when he realized he was helpless and was nothing without God. His passion for god's love was deep and sincere. He knew that his God, the heavenly Father was his hope. It was only in the silence of his troubled soul did he hear the voice of God.

What I have to discover is the wordless and total surrender of my heart in silence. It is here where my prayer becomes one with my heart. It is here that wordlessly I can invoke the name of Jesus in full wonder and love! It is here that tears and the fervour of my heart meet the divine heart that is more intimate to me than I am to myself! It is here that in this solitude do St Bernard words of alone with the alone makes sense. It is in this depth of spiritual bliss alone that I can feel the presence of Christ in the most inner chamber of my heart that produces a glow of intense pleasurably warmth of glorious tender love. It is here that I can fully appreciate St Augustine's maxim: May I know YOU; may I know myself! It is here that my prayer for mercy is heard as I cry out for help and lift up my hands towards his holy sanctuary [Psalm 28:2]. It is here that the love of God touches my heart – for we know how dearly God loves us, because he has given us the Holy Spirit to fill my heart with his love [Romans 5:5].

Thomas Merton in his booklet on Contemplative Prayer concludes without true contemplative aspirations, without a total love for God and an uncompromising thirst for his truth, religion tends in the end to become an opiate. To which I say Amen! Amen! No amount of silence and solitude will bring us closer to God if the love for him is not in our heart; like the drug addiction we will have our emotional high but no more! The beams to divine love that silence and solitude can channel will be non-existent.

I seek the path of the contemplative prayer for I passionately believe it is the way of divine truth and as the love of God touches my heart with all its tenderness, however little it may be, I feel more empowered than ever to be equally tender and compassionate in all my activities. I seek the path of silence and solitude, with all its challenges, for it is indeed the path to divine love. When the truth and love of God is discovered the unknowing cloud of divinity is not so unknowing; it is very lovable and divine!

Trust in the Lord and do good then you will live in safety in the land and prosper.
Take delight in the Lord and he will give you your heart's desires
Commit everything you do to the Lord
Trust him, and he will help you
Be still in the presence of the Lord, and wait patiently for him to act
[Psalm 37:3-5,7]

Lord Restore My Soul

THANKFUL HEART OF LIGHT COVERS THE BLADE OF DARKNESS

Give thanks to the Lord; for he is good; his love endures forever [Psalm 118:1]

The other night I was watching a Japanese Romeo and Juliet story where heartfelt love could not overcome the deep violent culture of their society. In the end Romeo martyred his life by letting Juliet kill him and she in turn destroyed her power so that her village would be saved from destruction. The message of this film is disturbing and even more so as we read of the constant violence throughout the globe. Yet at the same time thousands of families are gathering for the Thanksgiving weekend, where the sounds of music, joy and reunion laughter abounds; and the symbolic Turkey is stuffed and ate with gusto! This contrast to me is like the Tale of Two Cities; one is at war; the other is at peace! I cannot but help wonder whether the symphony of mankind is a constant battle between the tension of peace and the tyranny of power; where suffering is the great equalizer born out of love that breaks this conflict.

I wonder too how many families take a moment to reflect on the harmony of their society, the freedom of mobility, the freedom to express opinions; the freedom to choose their place in society and the freedom to simply have fun. By all means we need to be thankful for family but do we give one second to consider how precarious this freedom truly is when we consider the freedom lost in most of our world. A freedom that is lost when the Heart of love is under and bound by the Blade of violence because of our lust for power and greed! Instead of the Heart covering the blade of violence with love that is bled to bring the lover home!

Bountiful goods and all the desire for materialistic gains can never truly give us the peace we earnestly seek. There is always that spirit of darkness that haunts us where enough is not enough. Our hearts can never be fully thankful for desire for more keeps our hearts unsatisfied. We never really know what we had until it is lost! In such a state our words of thanksgiving can be shallow for the blade of darkness has stricken our hearts where the spirit of contentment and love has no place. But there is a way out of this darkness if we are prepared to walk into the light of truth where goodness and love endures forever.

The psalmist can sing of thankfulness and love for he knows the source of his life. He is the one who has created him! The one who guides him! The one who watches over him! The one who loves him! The one who knows his heart! He is not alone! His passion and depth of love for his Lord is unbounded. His heart beats with joy to follow his Lord; his heart beats with grief when he does not obey his Lord! The lover lives for his beloved. They are united as one!

This weekend as we give a moment to be thankful for family, home, health and friends, let our hearts not forget the source of our love- the suffering lamb who was slain for our sins. Let our hearts now sing with the psalmist: You are my God and I will give thanks; you are my God and I will exalt you. Give thanks to the Lord, for he is good; his love endures forever.

THE COMFORTER EMBRACES THE CONTROLLER

May your unfailing love be my comfort [Psalm 119:76ff] I will give them comfort and joy instead of sorrow [Jeremiah 31:13ff]. Blessed are those who mourn for they will be comforted. [Matthew 5:4]. The God of all comfort: who comforts us in all troubles so that we can comfort those in any trouble with the comfort we have received from God.[1 Corinthians 1:3-4ff] The Lord God said, "It is not good for man to be alone. I will make a helper suitable for him"[Genesis 2:18]

I was in one big huff. No one understood me. No one was listening to me. My mood was as dark as the gray blustering weather. I stormed out of the room; banging the door behind me. I ran up the twisting gravel path to the highest point of the tor. With panting breath I looked at the surging waves below; a mass of deep blue water that threatened to smash the rocks off the cliff with its almost demonic force and thunderous noise, as the white crest of the waves smashed against the rocks that sent salty spray afar and then with calmer force retreated to yet again to repeat the surge once more. As I stared at this hypnotic scene in awe of its power, I could hear the faint plaintive cries of the seagulls. When I looked up the black and grey cumulonimbus clouds were massing in the sky with great speed heralding the imminent storm; the wind was playing havoc with my hair and distorting my facial features and it took all my power to remain standing. Then with a gentle patter at first the rain drops came and within seconds they turned into a warm wet crescendo of water that drenched all they touched. I did not move. I felt a kindred spirit with this storm. The wind, the rain, the noise all represented the churning emotions within me. I was alone; but I was one with the storm. I connected with its fury. I yelled with frustration whose words were silenced by nature's force. Then without warning a streak of yellow light streaked out of the clouds to embrace me in full glory with its heat. Steam from my drying clothes covered me with a gentle mist. "David, I am here; you are not alone" whispered the voice within me. I was soothed with joy with these words. As I opened my eyes that had been closed because of the brightness of the Sun I saw the clouds vanishing leaving in its wake an emerald blue sky and a becalmed sea. Behind me I heard an anxious voice which I knew so well "David, Come Home! You will catch a cold"It was my mother. I smiled, "I am fine, mum" and turned towards her. But I wondered who was that voice within that comforted me in my time of need.

When love is lost; when distrust is born there is an urgent stirring in our soul to self-protect. The "angst" within percolates in our heart until the boiling point arrives and we simply explode our frustration, anger and rage. If this behaviour is left to grow unchecked not only bonding with others becomes nay impossible but what is worse, we fail to bond with our inner feelings. Our failure to resolve this loss will impair our ability to recognize and help others we care and love.

Likewise, any hope of intimacy that is desired so much is a distant hope and no more! We live an isolated life that is dark, stormy lacking in hope, and one that is expressed in silent torment. Rage, we hold is our controller. It is our protector. It is our fortress. It is the very antithesis of love! The consequence is we live by keeping a distance from ourselves. We are indeed an island of utter misery surrounded by a sea of doubt and darkness.

This goes against God's desire. We are created for love, for enduring relationships. Why is it then we men when under stress who need help fail to ask whereas women have no trouble seeking help. Pride is too simple an answer. I truly believe men relationally do not know how to connect whereas women are awesome at connection. The Lord God said, "It is not good for man to be alone. I will make a helper suitable for him. Women indeed are incredible helpers. They know how to console, to reassure, to soothe and to love. Men fail to connect because the great controller Rage does not permit him to look inside of himself for help and support. This is a truism for the independent man who cannot recognize and care for his needs for intimacy cannot recognize and care for the community.

Yet there is hope. Our Lord has given us the Great Comforter his Holy Spirit that through the work of the Trinity teaches the love of God and the compassion of Jesus. It is through the church that the community of love and hope grows! It is through the church that we can learn to take responsibility for our feelings; to be shown how to love ourselves, to cherish ourselves, to know we are special and are beloved. To know that we live alone we belong to the family of God; a family of compassion, of service and of empathy. The more we love ourselves a strange thing starts to happen, we desire to give love rather than to get love. It is the sharing of our love that breaks down the loneliness. That is why I believe the Holy Spirit, the great comforter, will embrace the Controller, our state of rage and tenderize it to one of compassionate love. If the Church is faithful in God's mission of love the Church will ever endure.

The need is great for in North America 5 million kids are annually traumatized emotionally and violently. In Syria alone there are 2 million kids daily traumatized by a non ending war. With singleness growing it is not surprising that a spirit of loneliness is well entrenched. In a recent study in the UK there are over one million kids without a father; and there is a place near Liverpool where two thirds of the kids have never known a Dad!

   I earnestly pray with all my heart that the Church will continue to be relevant where the Spirit of love exists and is known as a community that is safe and secure. Jesus said "Let the little children come to me" I pray that the church will remain the place where lost can come and rest their head on the altar of love where the Spirit of love will caress them with the warmth of compassion and hope!

THE GIFT OF LIFE IS GOD'S LOVE TO US

*Please hurry, Lord, and answer my prayer
I feel hopeless.
Don't turn away and leave me here to die.
Each morning let me learn more about your love because I trust you.
I come to you in prayer, asking for your guidance (Psalm 143:7-8)
I am your servant.*

Whenever I read this psalm I am reminded of a time in my life where there was a deep feeling of hopelessness; I really thought I was going to die! I did not know it until much later that the hand of God was on my shoulder guiding and calming my tense nerves.

I was 19 years old, in my spare time I worked with a Pastor whose church was the streets of the local gangs. It was in a large urban city in the middle of England. There was much poverty, anger and gang rivalry. This was the time of the Rockers and Mods. The Rockers were the motor- cycle gangs; leather, long hair and chains were always worn. The Mods rode the scooters, tight pants and Beatles like suit and metal rods were their constant apparel! They detested each other. The Pastor vision was to keep the peace, to befriend them and bring them to the Lord. On this particular day we received a call that "a rumble" was to take place by the river. "Come on, David" and without a thought I scrambled after him and jumped into his Volkswagen "Beetle Bug". When we arrived at the scene my hands started to sweat. On one side of the bridge were the Rockers with the chains out; and on the other side were the Mods with their roads in their hands. To my horror the pastor drove through the gap and parked his car in the centre and to my dismay he left me in the car as he ambled to the Rockers. In an instant the Mods moved forward surrounding the car with me trembling inside. This was no long fun! I was trapped in the car! My life was totally in the hands of these frenzied hooligans. I put a brave face and looked out of the front window. I saw in their faces fear. A spirit of calmness filled my soul. I recognized some of the guys. With a calmness I did not feel, I called the names of the Mods I knew and asked "what's up" My fear dissipated as the Mods started to smile and meet me like a "brother". Love your neighbour as God has loved you was given a sharp meaning that night!

While it has taken a life journey. I am eager each morning to learn more about God and to discover what he has in store for me. His word is powerful. It needs no interpretation, just action. If it feels God has abandoned me it is because I have sinned; it is I who has abandoned him. He is a patient God because of his love for me. He has taught me the true meaning of love and honesty. He is there to pick me up when I fall. He has shown me the way of love and has tenderly removed my fears, "my enemy".

The physical scars of my life disappear before God's grace but the scars of the heart still beat strongly from time to time. I am convinced that they will eventually be swallowed up by the gentle grace of His Spirit. What I do know whatever scars, bruises, humiliation and fears I have experienced none of them exceed the pain and torture that our Saviour Jesus Christ experienced on the Cross to save our lives from sin. This to me is a supreme act of love that is beyond my human understanding. All I can do for this Hope of Eternal Life is to simply bow down and worship him with all my might and strength that is in my soul for He has given me the Gift of Life! May I use this gift wisely! This will occur, if like the psalmist, I pray each day to the Lord that I may learn and remain on the path of love.

Each morning let me learn more about your love because I trust you. I come to you in prayer, asking for your guidance. Let me not lose sight of your compassion and love. O, Lord this is indeed the Gift of Life.

THE PATH OF LOVE

It is the Lord who has strengthened the steps of man and chooses his path; though he may stumble, he will not fall for the Lord upholds him with his hand. [Psalm 37:23-24]. Put your hope in the Lord and follow his paths [Psalm 37:34] I will maintain my love to him forever and my covenant with him will never fail. [Psalm 89:28].

There is nothing that gives me more pleasure than to hike on a new trail. The more twists and turns, the greater the ups and downs of the path are an awesome delight. The diverse vegetation and the variety of birds seen; all remind me of our Creator Lord. I can relax when I walk this path. I know where I am going; if the path is well worn and there are signs, I am reminded where I am. All I need to do is enjoy the presence of "being" which I do with gusto. The path is my beacon. I sometimes, wonder if I stray off this path and make my own path would I be so relaxed, for there is always the possibility I might become lost.

Especially if there are no signs to give you indication of direction! So, it is with my soul. I find I cannot live in a vacuum, or in a state of directionlessness. I find I need to search for the Lord to give me direction. He is the one who soothes me and comforts me, when I stumble and through his mercy and love I find that he strengthens my soul. For this to happen I need to be on the "chosen" path.

My ears have to be attentive to his whispers, my heart has to be open to receive his grace and correction and my soul must desire to be faithful in love to him. In short, the spirit of "hesed" has to infill me with joy and hope of his covenant. Just as the path of the forest reminds me of the direction I need to walk; so. do I need to be reminded of the covenants of the Lord so I can walk the path of salvation. Just as the gentle movement of tree tops cools me in the hot summer days; so, does the gentle inner whispering of the Holy Spirit soothe me in times of trouble; for God's love is persistent!

It is a love that is beyond human reason. I am in awe that he still loves me when I am so fickle. It is a love that expects obedience to his word. It is a love that consists of self-giving, trust, deep affection and joyful submission to the Law. Just as a forest cannot be known without the trees and the bushes; so the true knowledge of God cannot be separated from love for him. This "hesed" love of Hebrew time is not based on feeling; it is based on a decision of will. It is a commitment to fulfill a promise, a covenant of love. How different is the spirit of "agape" love in the New Testament; it is sacrificial and unconditional. "God loved the world so much; he gave his only

Son, so that everyone who believes in him may not perish but have eternal life –[John 3:16]. Because of Jesus Christ's ultimate sacrifice, we can receive divine grace. God's chosen path in Hebrew Time was the path of "hesed" based on obedience. Now God's path is "Agape" based on unmerited grace. Which path I wonder am I on? The path of loving obedience or the path of unmerited grace where I can – Love one another as he loves me!

TOO BUSY TO LISTEN

Hear, O my people and I will warn you- if you would listen to me (Psalm 81:8)
But my people would not listen to me (Psalm 81:11)
If my people would but listen to me Psalm (81.13)

On one of those sultry summer mornings; I remember with much delight standing on the golden sands of Long Beach. My toes were being tickled by the fine sand grains. My hair was blown constantly over my face as the early dawn wind guests blew over me. Wisps of morning fog drifted towards the coast to be evaporated by the sun's heat. White Seagulls glided over me shrieking with such fervour that peace was shattered almost overcoming the diminishing roar of the outgoing waves. With one swoop they landed on the exposed sand to enjoy the inevitable feast that follows the withdrawing waters. In an instance masses of sandpipers flying in aerobatic precision joined the seagulls. Small crabs could be seen diving into the sand to avoid becoming breakfast! The tranquillity of the beach had gone with the constant cries from the melee of birds as they fought over their food. As I looked up past the blue green sea with their white foamed capped waves, I could see the spout of water erupting from a hunting Orca whale hunting stealthily for the seal! The sky was a sapphire blue promising another hot day. To my right and left shining from the receding waters was the beach rocks covered with all kinds of mussels and sea shell creature; the anemones opening up displaying their deadly gold, red and purple tentacles as if in homage to the glory of the Sun! The beauty of this scene left me in awe of the wonder of God's creation. What joy of peace did I feel! A sense of mystic sereneness caressed my soul! The beach I was standing on has been here for eons of years before me and will continue to be so in the future. Yet there is sadness for God's creation is step by step is being eroded by un- listening generations. This is the underlying message of Psalm 81 which is very apt for our times.

Listen! Listen! Listen! 3 times the psalmist warns the people to listen. They are warned if you refuse God laws then foreign gods will come and you will become sent in exile and enslaved. This will lead to loss of freedoms, left to your own narcissistic whims and darkness. There will be much poverty, famine and destruction; which can be reversed if we would only listen. So why don't we? One reason is the cult of materialism that provides all needs with a push of button! Convenience is the path to happiness and prosperity. In our shells of individualism and selfies who cares about our neighbour. Who worries that the climate is warming, that species are on the verge of extinction, that our pollution is destroying the waters; for in the comfort of our cocoon homes this is of no concern of mine. So we become deaf to the cries of the helpless, we become indifferent to the needs of the oppressed and we become deaf to our Lord and Creator.

While the psalmist expresses with delight and joy for all the things that our God has created and done; he sombrely warns of the danger of God's judgement on those who refuse to turn back on their secular folly of existence and turn in repentance to face God and to obey and listen to his Word! In blindness they have forgotten that a Day of Judgment will come. When it does they will wish they had not been so busy to just listen to the word of God! It will be too late!

TRUST IS THE OPEN DOOR TO GOD'S PEACE!

My days disappear like smoke,
And my bones are burning through in a furnace.
I am wasting away like grass and my appetite is gone.
My groaning never stops and my bones can be seen through my skin.
I am like a lonely owl in the desert or a restless sparrow on a roof.
My life fades like a shadow at the end of the day and withers like grass
Psalm 102:3-7, 11

Can you not feel the pain, the isolation and the depression expressed in these words? Who has not at some time in our lives felt the darkness within our souls; where all seems lost and life seems so futile and meaningless! Just to exist has become a burden. Complaining and groaning has become the daily manta. To me this is the consequence of a lonely heart that has not found peace; and is slowly withering and dying; with each beat sounding the walk of the dancing dead! It is so easy to laugh at this absurd insane existence but there are many such "lost souls" who walk in the Valley of darkness and fail to see the light reflected on the top of the summit! These people live in a prison of self-condemnation where joy, love and hope have gone amiss!

In my search for love I live in a turbulent see-saw between love and despondency; between gratitude and sadness; between longing and indifference and between light and darkness. What is truly amazing the moment I start to walk in the valley of darkness there is that spiritual pull that whispers: Come David, you are loved. Do not fear. I am with you. Instantly there is a feeling of warmth that washes through me and the desire to hold, to belong and to open my heart takes hold. But alas that dark spirit within me calls me back –Don't be foolish. Have you not learnt that love is dangerous; it is not trustworthy. It is better for you to look to yourself! I do what I ought not to do and a sense of indifference and isolation pervades my soul as I emotionally detach myself.

The curse in my life is that I do not trust. That is my heart is not open to trust. Is it no wonder that relationships are often sparse and distant! Not because I desire to do this' but rather it is because I deflect the possibility of love to enter my heart because of my distrustful demeanour. Is it any wonder my heart belongs to the "Lonely heart" Club! This often leads to anger and frustrations for I know that I am robbing and sabotaging any hope of love in my life. All I am left with is to moan and complain!

Why does detachment come so easily and faultlessly into my actions? Was it lack of love in my early life? Why when I desire love so much; I do my best to avoid it? What is it I fear? I believe it centers on me not loving myself enough and not trusting God enough. I am my own worst critic. In truth I have a very difficult time in accepting I am a child of God and that I am blessed; experience has shown otherwise. The good news is God is working in my life for the words that –you are my son, you are my child, you are loved are gently tenderizing my heart to allow grace and mercy into my soul. It is a long journey!

I am learning the true meaning of love. Love can hurt, but in this suffering forgiveness and peace can endure. But there is still that sadness I still walk the peripheral of community more as an observer than participant. I constantly pray that before I leave this earth I will truly belong. Peace in my heart will have found its home! My restless search for Love is no more as I rest in the arms of the Shepherd's embrace!

WHAT IS PRAYER?

Cleanse me from these hidden faults. Keep your servant from deliberate sins! Don't let them control me. Then I will be free of guilt and innocent of great sin. May the words of my mouth and the meditation of my heart be pleasing to you, O my Lord, my rock and redeemer. (Psalm 19:12-14)

The act of praying is to address God with adoration, confession, supplication, thanksgiving in a spirit of intercessory love. Prayer in its purest form is an expression of love for our Lord and our love for our neighbour. For me this is often difficult to do for my mind is constantly processing ideas and working out conceptual thoughts that the heart is marginalized to the borders of my passionate desires. It is necessary for me to find a place of quiet and solitude where I can focus on hearing the word of God whispering into my soul. I love the imagery of Paul in his letter to the Ephesians where he prepares himself to speak to his Father in heaven:

My response is to get down on my knees before the Father, this magnificent Father who parcels out all heaven and earth. I ask him to strengthen you by his spirit – not a brute strength but a glorious inner strength – that Christ will live in you as you open the door and invite him in. And I ask him that with both feet planted firmly on love, you'll be able to take in with all Christians the extravagant dimensions of Christ's love. Reach out and experience the breadth! Test its length! Plumb the depths! Rise to the heights! Live full lives, full in the fullness of God. God can do anything, you know – far more than you could ever imagine or guess or request in your wildest dreams! He does it not by pushing us around by working within us, his Spirit deeply and gently within us. [Ephesians 3:14-21 The Message].

Notice the gentle words of adoration Paul has for his Father in heaven and the intercessory focus of the prayer. It is a prayer of a lover to his beloved. It is a prayer that focuses on the "thou" not the "I". It is a prayer of one who knows his Father: A Father that blesses his son; a son who exalts his Father. It is a heartfelt prayer of deep passion and conviction! It is a prayer where the divine and the human connect to produce a world of tenderness and love! It is a prayer that I often seek but seldom discover.

Paradoxically prayer is communication with God; but often God is hidden. Not because God desires to be but because he cannot enter my heart as it is not pure. Only when my heart has confessed its faults and received the forgiveness of my sins through God's mercy and grace will God appear to me. When he still remains hidden and words fail me all I can cry: How can I know all the sins lurking in my heart?

Cleanse me from these hidden faults. Keep your servant from deliberate sins! Don't let them control me. Then I will be free of guilt and innocent of great sin. May the words of my mouth and the meditation of my heart be pleasing to you, O my Lord, my rock and redeemer. [Psalm 19:12-14]. Through silence and solitude I wait for the whisper of God to enter my heart and when the word comes I feel the warmth of God's love entangling my heart with a tender love and compassion that is beyond words! With joy I know I am not alone but am blessed by his presence!

Times such as these are few. Oh! The aroma of experiencing the touch of God is enough to restore my faith and eternal love for him. The words of St Patrick spring forth with more vigour and certainty in my love of my Saviour:

I arise today
Through God's strength to pilot me,
God's might to uphold me
God's wisdom to guide me
God's eye to look before me
God's ear to hear me
God's word to speak to me
God hand to guide me
God's shield to protect me
From snares of devils
From temptation of vices
From everyone who wish me ill afar and near
[St Patrick's Breastplate]

When I speak to another person I use my mouth;

but when I speak to God it is through my heart. When the heart is cold so is my prayer. When my heart boils for the love of God my prayer is alive with passion and ecstatic awe of his blessed love for me! All I can do is cry out Yes Lord I will arise and follow you.

The sadness in such moments of joy is fleeting and my heart yearns for the heart to be rekindled with the fire of love once more. It is this desire: this yearning if you will that keeps me praying for God's presence.

As a seeker of God's love I know it will be my life's journey to be the Prodigal Son seeking my Father's embrace. I know that prayer is the way to the Father's home. It is the culmination of a life journey of faith, trial and love.

Prayer is indeed the channel that bonds God's blessed love for me to the love that pulsates with eager beats in my heart to embrace that divine love that can only result in – Yes, Lord I arise to follow you!

WISDOM OF LOVING SILENCE

I said "I will watch my ways and keep my tongue from sin; I will put a muzzle on my mouth as long as the wicked are in my presence" [Psalm 39:1] But now Lord, what do I look for? My hope is in you. [Psalm 39:7].O Lord, hear my prayer. Listen to my cry for mercy. Teach me to do your will, for you are my God; may your spirit lead me on the level ground. [Psalm 143:1, 10] Who will separate us from the love of Christ?..No in all things we are conquerors through him who loved us. [Romans 8:35, 37]

There are times I wish I could recall the words I have spoken out of frustration and anger; that caused more harm than good. In the midst of a passionate turmoil my spirit of pride and a desire for vengeance tends to overcome the spirit of love and reconciliation. My tongue became a weapon of torment as I spoke words of discontent instead of words of love and compassion. It would have been far better for me to have remained silent. Wait quietly for the presence of the Lord to provide guidance and discernment. But now, like the psalmist, I must seek the Lord and ask for his forgiveness, through repentance and reconciliation.

When a fracture occurs in a relationship because of a wrong word spoken; a trust is betrayed and it takes time for healing to take place. The ground, so to speak, has become bumpy and uncertain. I have discovered it takes patience to restore the relationship to a level ground. This patience is learnt by living and understanding what it means to live under the will of God. What is this will of God- That we should "Love one another as I have loved you"; Love is patient, love is kind, it does not envy, it does not boast, it is not proud. It is not rude, it is not self-seeking, it is not easily angered, and it keeps no record of wrongs. Love does not delight in evil but rejoice with the truth. It always protects, always trusts, always hopes, and always perseveres.

It is through the practice of reading, praying and contemplating on the words of our Lord that we learn what it means to live in God's will. It is an act of love and joy; it is not just an act of conformity and obedience. The act of love and joy comes from the heart that desires to be filled with God's spirit of unmerited grace; this is the way our soul is transformed from the inside out. Our union with God strengthens as our love for him grows more intense. This love protects in times of testing and trials. God is with us as God is within us. Whereas the act of conformity tends to change our external action but not our heart; for love is often absent. We are ill prepared to face the trials and tests of life which can easily overwhelm us. It is imperative that we seek and truly believe that God is our Hope.

God is love

Lord Restore My Soul

Made in the USA
Middletown, DE
30 March 2021